REWILDING

# REWILDING

## POEMS FOR THE ENVIRONMENT

CRYSTAL S. GIBBINS
EDITOR

Flexible Press
Minneapolis, Minnesota
2020

COPYRIGHT © 2020 Flexible Press
www.flexiblepub.com

ISBN 978-1-7339763-4-3

Editor: Crystal S. Gibbins
Cover design: Crystal S. Gibbins

Environmental consciousness is important to us. This book is printed with chlorine-free ink and acid-free paper stock supplied by a Forest Stewardship Council certified provider. The paper stock is made from 30% post-consumer waste recycled material.

**About Flexible Press**: Flexible Press is dedicated to supporting authors, communities, and mission-driven non-profits through story. Somewhere between some and all of the profits from Flexible Press titles are donated to relevant nonprofits. Find out more at www.flexiblepub.com.

# TABLE OF CONTENTS

Without love of the land, conservation
lacks meaning or purpose, for only in
a deep and inherent feeling for the land
can there be dedication in preserving it.
~ Sigurd F. Olson

My introduction to the wilderness and conservation came at a young age. For my family, living on the remote islands in Lake of the Woods (Ontario and Minnesota), we were constantly reminded of the four-season symphony of the lake and the rhythms of nature.

Most days began with a mix chorale of birds and the piping of frogs. My brother and I would walk down to the dock and peer through the wooden planks to watch minnows dart and crayfish scuttle along the rocks below. Sometimes we heard a muskrat or an otter splutter through the reeds and crash blindly into the water. We spent hours watching eagles kite the sky, beavers and pelicans chug along the shoreline like tugboats, and, if we were fortunate enough, a blue heron or moose would appear mysteriously out of the morning fog to greet us.

And we were reminded that the lake is full of nutrients and medicines, too. We learned how to swim, canoe, forage for berries, onions, and mushrooms, harvest wild rice, process maple syrup, and, above all else, how to be good land and water stewards—a knowledge and ethic passed down by our Ojibwe and Métis ancestors. I did not know at the time how privileged we were to have birds, fish, trees, and so many other wild creatures as companions to our childhood days on the lake, but as I grow older I realize how deeply and profoundly Lake of the Woods has shaped and defined my identity, values, and perspective of the world. This waterscape will always be home—it is in my DNA.

Although I now reside on the south shore of Lake Superior, nestled between Chequamegon Bay and the Chequamegon-Nicolet National Forest, I still make the long trip north to Lake of the Woods several times a year, a nine-hour trek through the Twin Ports and Iron Range, over the Laurentian Divide, along Superior National Forest and Voyagers National Park, and across the border into Canada, where I park my vehicle at the landing and jump into a boat bound for the islands. The idea for this anthology began to germinate some time along this route of rugged terrain—a region that is idyllic and serene to the casual passerby, but it is also a place inflicted by environmental degradation and haunted by cultural traumas to this day.

Originally, *Rewilding* was going to be a book centering on northern Minnesota and the Boundary Waters Canoe Area Wilderness (BWCAW), as a directive to safeguard these watersheds and wild habitats from sulfide-ore copper mining, deforestation, and further destruction to the ecosystem. While the thematic focus has broadened to explore natural environments and ecological crises beyond Minnesota, the borderlands and boundary waters remain as a literal and figurative vein running through and between many of these poems.

This anthology features a considerable range of voices, styles, and approaches from a diverse group of contemporary poets. Readers will find poems that are explicitly activist in their political dimensions, some more implicitly so, raising ethical and epistemological questions about responsibility and community. Marybeth Holleman, Craig Santos Perez, Vivian Faith Prescott, and Cintia Santana write poems of melting glaciers and address the fragility of the planet. Other poems emphasize a needed corrective and encourage sustainability. Karen Solie's and Julia Spicher Kasdorf's poetry blend satire and wry humor with environmental concerns, and poems by Heidi Lynn Staples and Juan J. Morales revel in ironic opulence. There are poems of natural and human-instigated disasters. Poems of praise and admiration for birds, fish, mammals, and insects. Poets like Ted Kooser and Thomas R. Smith examine the smallest of creatures and encourage us to reevaluate our relationship with the nonhuman world, while Joy Harjo communicates a desire for renewal and balance, both spiritually and environmentally.

Though the selection of poems in *Rewilding* is not comprehensive of contemporary poets writing about the environment, it is my hope that this anthology will stimulate positive change and inspire new writers, leaders, and land stewards to conserve, repair, restore, and protect natural processes and wilderness areas.

Crystal Spring Gibbins
*Washburn, Wisconsin*

# ACKNOWLEDGMENTS

I would like to extend my appreciation and gratitude to the spirited citizens of Friends of the Boundary Waters Wilderness and their allies who give their time and hearts to educating the public, addressing critical issues that impact the environment and neighboring communities, and preserving the Boundary Waters for future generations. I am grateful for the species, landscapes, and waterscapes that manage, against all odds, to regenerate themselves each year.

I am especially indebted to the *Split Rock Review* editors—Amy Clark, Whitney Jacobson, Andrew Jones, and Adrian Gibbons Koesters—whose brilliance and friendship I deeply value. Thank you so much for your generosity, knowledge, and help reading hundreds of poems for this anthology. And to my publisher, Bill Burleson and the team at Flexible Press, thank you for your enthusiasm in this project, your unwavering support, and bringing this book into the world.

I wish to acknowledge and thank the poets and presses who granted permission to reprint poems, some of whom were generous to waive fees. Your poems nourish these pages.

I give a heartfelt thanks to my husband, Joshua Schloesser, for his support as a sounding board of ideas, comments on my drafts, and patience during the prolonged hours I spent reading and writing at my desk.

And a very special thanks goes to my parents, Dan and Sheri Gibbins, for instilling a sense of wonder and for being my first guides into the wilderness.

## Boundary Waters

Off the road
where lichen and thick moss
take in minerals
beneath the balsam
over the border
past the landing
in the stone face of granite
above the water's mirror
small islands where
root dives into stone
amid broken limbs
of white pine
behind the reflection of day
into dark endings
reached for my own reaching
hand in the cold water
of October—
a tail flick of a fin
among the sunken
shoulders
in a vein of ore.
To take from another body
is a question
answered by loon
or by the morning rime
with weasel
searching the char of a cold fire.
After the urgent
animal of the body—
a heavy frost
and the moose that trod
over our path
running, hunted.

# In the Water Filled Mine Pit

*After "Mine Songs" by Sara Pajunen*

In the boat on the water, I slide over her body, the excavation. She is slag. She is crushed stone. Unburied. I am over her bones, geologic, Mesabi iron. I drift over knee and shin and float over her shattered self, heaped upon the earth. Over boulders submerged. Veins were broken open, emptied and made into freight.

A cold current from the drift presses against the chamber. The bow lifts. She is bedrock, the bottom of the continent and through her runs dark and invisible rivers without shore. She is the Divide. In the seams of the tectonic plates, she is lit with dynamite and extracted, mined, carried by trains to the ships. I see a shoulder of iron. In place of her head, a deep shaft.

Remade, she becomes steel, becomes bridge, becomes beam. Ship and tank and weapon. At the end, junk in the junkyards rusting into the weeds.

∧

The vessel turns like the needle of a compass broken from its post. I hear the tail splash of a trout. The fish spiral along the perimeter inside the pit on a winding road once traveled, in shifts, by men in hard hats in old dump trucks and steam shovels. The trout tend the broken cables. Skeletal and rusted frames.

Surface tensions. A fence cannot hold back the danger. The water has risen. The engineers call it water gain: precipitation, surface water inflow, a rise in the water table, a threat the walls of the pit. Light falls but can't find bottom three hundred feet below. Circles tumble and bend beneath the water's surface. I hear the gravel sliding in. I hear insects and bird wings over the factory of the deep.

∧

No shore, the place only steep. Stained with ore, the water feels like ice. It magnifies the hand that I plunge beneath the surface. It breaks the lines of my body, her body. The vessel falls upward. The ore could condense into the red mist of atoms. I break the surface and sink. I break the surface and rise.

## AIMEE NEZHUKUMATATHIL

### Mr. Cass and the Crustaceans

Whales the color of milk have washed ashore
in Germany, their stomachs clogged full
of plastic and car parts. Imagine the splendor
of a creature as big as half a football field—

the magnificence of the largest brain
of any animal—modern or extinct. I have
been trying to locate my fourth grade
science teacher for years. Mr. Cass, who

gave us each a crawfish he found just past
the suburbs of Phoenix, before strip malls
licked every good desert with a cold blast
of Freon and glass. Mr. Cass who played

soccer with us at recess, who let me check
on my wily, snappy crawfish in the plastic
blue pool before class started so I could place
my face to the surface of the water and see

if it still skittered alive. I hate to admit
how much this meant to me, the only brown girl
in the classroom. How I wish I could tell Mr. Cass
how I've never stopped checking the waters—

the ponds, the lakes, the sea. And I worry
that I've yet to see a sperm whale, except when
they beach themselves in coves. How many songs
must we hear from the sun-bleached bones

of a seabird or whale? If there were anyone on earth
who would know this, Mr. Cass, it's you—how even
bottle caps found inside a baby albatross corpse
can make a tiny ribcage whistle with the ocean wind

blows through it just right—I know wherever you are,
you'd weep if you heard this sad music. I think
how you first taught us kids how to listen to water,
and I'm grateful for each story in its song.

# TED KOOSER

## A Mouse Nest

It had been built in my band saw, inside the steel housing,
two halves like a shirt box on end, with a lid to unfasten,
exposing the pulleys and blade, a perilous place for a nest,
a couple of fistfuls of yellow fiberglass insulation
brought from afar, wad by wad, and neatly packed into
the spokes of a pulley that hadn't been spun for a while,
although now I was hoping to use it, to cut out a fiberboard
seat for a chair that a two-year-old visitor had climbed on,
putting a foot through the caning. I suspected there might
be a nest: there were fiberglass tufts that had fallen out onto
the saw's metal table. So, before switching it on, I unfastened
the housing to look. There was the nest, exposed to the light,
big as a softball, split and flattened to fit that tight space,
and dirty, too, like cotton candy somebody had dropped
on a midway. It all looked unoccupied, nobody at home,
my whole workshop now holding its breath, then it stirred,
and out pushed the whiskery nose and shiny black eyes
of a mouse, which then, face to face with its tormentor
drew back in that innocent fiberglass cloud with no sign
of a storm building inside. I picked up a wood shim
that lay handy, and stealthily started to pick away pieces.
At first there was no sign of life, but as I worked in toward
the center I sensed pandemonium building, the kind
you'd see when a storm-warning siren far in the distance
starts insisting a tornado's coming, and suddenly that
mother mouse bolted for safety, four mouselets aboard,
hanging onto her nipples, all of them slipping and sliding
down the back side of the housing, tumbling out on the floor,

scrabbling for purchase, the whole load dragging into
the shadows beyond, but for one who had either let go
or pulled loose and fallen away, a mouse in miniature,
about the size of a brazil nut, with sleek gray fur and ears
too small to hear much, eyes so tiny or so tightly closed
I couldn't see them, nor, I supposed, could they see me.
I left it where it fell and picked out the rest of the nest,
which was pissy and warm at its middle, put back the saw's
housing—a housing indeed!—and cut out the chair seat
while beneath me, between my enormous brown shoes
the mouse feebly kicked with its back feet, trying to push
the overturned boat of itself under the edge of a toolbox,
the thin oars of its forelegs stretching to pat at the floor,
and when I had finished my work I turned out the light
and left it there in its predicament, adrift on a sea
of despair no bigger than a jar lid. Hours later, before
going to bed, I walked down to my workshop to look,
and snapped on the overhead light, and entered the stillness,
where every trace of what had happened to us there
was gone, except for a little red fiberboard sawdust.

## Conch Shell

Neither of them had ever seen
an ocean, but a cousin who had
brought back a conch shell
that they kept among the dishes
in a glassed-front china cabinet.
It was pearly, pink and white
like the Royal Doulton cups
and saucers, but it looked more
like a gravy boat, with a spout
from which a boy could pour
the rush of an ocean into his ear.
But it wasn't the song of the waves
that charmed me, but distance,
all of that distance coiled inside,
at least a thousand miles of it,
not tightly wound, but loosely,
spiraling into the darkness
like the spring in a clock, a spring
that rang with ocean music.
I wanted to go, and I want to go
now, to make myself small,
and then smaller and smaller
and crawl all the way to the start,
then step out into the other side,
into a brightening room in the past,
holding a shell in my hands
to show them the ocean was there.

## Ode to Dirt

Dear dirt, I am sorry I slighted you,
I thought that you were only the background
for the leading characters—the plants
and animals and human animals.
It's as if I had loved only the stars
and not the sky which gave them space
in which to shine. Subtle, various,
sensitive, you are the skin of our terrain,
you're our democracy. When I understood
I had never honored you as a living
equal, I was ashamed of myself,
as if I had not recognized
a character who looked so different from me,
but now I can see us all, made of the
same basic materials—
cousins of that first exploding from nothing—
in our intricate equation together. O dirt,
help us find ways to serve your life,
you who have brought us forth, and fed us,
and who at the end will take us in
and rotate with us, and wobble, and orbit.

## LYNN DOMINA

### Do Carnivorous Plants Experience Hunger?

This carnivorous bladderwort floats,
rootless, like a dead stem
dropped from a weakened tree, its own leaves
dark as fleas, though the water fleas
it eats, if it can be said to eat,
are often translucent, crustaceous, and always
female. An entirely female
species has, honestly, a certain appeal,
though I would not want
to see through a woman's shell
to her wormy intestine or heavy brood pouch
bursting with swollen eggs. Bladderwort
reproduce in the usual way—sepals,
petals, stamens, seeds. In the usual way, they transform
sunlight into energy but sometimes
need surplus nitrogen or carbon, as I
occasionally need more
protein or sugar. I would say to the bladderwort
if it had an eardrum, a hammer, anvil, stirrup,
cochlea, even a curve of cartilage or earlobe—I would say
that carnivorous plants are unnatural,

defying order, the taxonomic tree of life, but of course
they are natural, for we find them
impersonating a thunderstorm's detritus when we wander
to a pond, hungry for a bit of nature, if only
nature weren't so wet and muddy, if only
its terrain were better groomed,
but I don't say
any of this because I remember those
people who have called me unnatural, dismayed
at my preference for a species of females, my intrigue
with these animals—clownfish, parrotfish, water fleas in dry weather—
that change sex to survive, my fascination
with these plants created to digest
both light and muscle.

# ADA LIMÓN

### Dandelion Insomnia

The big-ass bees are back, tipsy, sun drunk
and heavy with thick knitted leg warmers
of pollen. I was up all night again so today's
yellow hours seem strange and hallucinogenic.
The neighborhood is lousy with mowers, crazy
dogs, and people mending what winter ruined.
What I can't get over is something simple, easy:
How could a dandelion seed head seemingly
grow overnight? A neighbor mows the lawn
and bam, the next morning, there's a hundred
dandelion seed heads straight as arrows
and proud as cats high above any green blade
of manicured grass. It must bug some folks,
a flower so tricky it can reproduce asexually,
making perfect identical selves, bam, another me
bam, another me. I can't help it—I root
for that persecuted rosette so hyper in its
own making it seems to devour the land.
Even its name, translated from the French
*dent de lion*, means lion's tooth. It's vicious,
made for a time that requires tenacity, a way
of remaking the toughest self while everyone
else is asleep.

## Daisies

Go ahead: say what you're thinking. The garden
is not the real world. Machines
are the real world. Say frankly what any fool
could read in your face: it makes sense
to avoid us, to resist
nostalgia. It is
not modern enough, the sound the wind makes
stirring a meadow of daisies: the mind
cannot shine following it. And the mind
wants to shine, plainly, as
machines shine, and not
grow deep, as, for example, roots. It is very touching,
all the same, to see you cautiously
approaching the meadow's border in early morning,
when no one could possibly
be watching you. The longer you stand at the edge,
the more nervous you seem. No one wants to hear
impressions of the natural world: you will be
laughed at again; scorn will be piled on you.
As for what you're actually
hearing this morning: think twice
before you tell anyone what was said in this field
and by whom.

# MARY QUADE

## Bunnies

In the hallowed shade of basil and beneath the bower
of beans. What do you mean, to be so softly
ruinous? A puff, still as some mute memory
of illicit gnawing I'd like to forget. The dewy
after-chew of missing lettuce, the abrupt
halt of the tulip stalk, budless. I can forgive
your hunger, but not your choices. In the
straw mulch, I uncover a cuddled squirm of fur, all
eyes squinted shut against the view of my
cruel hesitation. Each ball of bunny nubbled
with ears, paws, nose. And somewhere, growing inside
jaws—teeth. You live this life acutely. Quiet and
aquiver, nibbling against the hawk, the fox, the boot,
the dog—in whose own sharp mouth you seem to sing.

## Octopus

Is everything shaped by what it
escapes? The octopus has no bones,
no rigid obstacle to conversion. Its head,
a sack of organs. Its arms,
nervous. Given a slit, it will
slip through, as one in a New Zealand aquarium
slid, forsaking the lid of its tank, squeezing
out of the glass box, then easing this new
idea of itself onto the floor, to the drain,
that door to the ocean. My pulpy brain
inside the stone of my skull shifts
between octopuses and octopi, depending
on the situation. The skin of the octopus
transforms to rock, to reef, to shadow-
dappled sand. Every octopus is an orphan
and lonely, breeding only once, then
dying. The female hangs on until
her eggs hatch—forgoing food, waving
sighs of currents over her brood. Somewhere
in Kansas, a little boy swallows a tiny octopus
and chokes—his caregiver, arrested for abuse.
The story flits through the murky news, then
disappears. Above the Bosphorus Strait, we
bite bits of suction cups bathed in
lemon juice and watch dolphins leap below,
stitching across the surface of the shipping lane—
a lucky and vulnerable sight, but we don't
know this. The octopus has eight limbs
and two hearts, like we do sometimes. In our
own sea, we hide, obscured
by squirts of ink. Just think, if you put an
octopus inside a jar, it can slowly
unscrew its way free.

## To Bear

The polar bear is threatened—
on a list of things you shouldn't
stuff into your suitcase
and carry across a border.
The polar bear is threatening
to melt, like tissue, into the sea.
You can't capture
with infrared film a well-fed bear, its
fire hid by fat and fur;
only hot breath appears,
bearless, an untranslated
warning. The polar bear
treads around the ice, sniffs for holes
where seals pop up for air, snaps
its jaws. There's a photo
of a man's head with scalp stripped off,
skull raw and spared.
A walrus is twice the size, but
this means nothing to me. What do trees
missed by lightning know? I know
only the bear in the small zoo,
chaos or cosmos of concrete,
always the pole of day
opposite the pole of night.
A window opens to the pool,
where the bear turns metronomical laps,
paw pushing off near my face,
again and again the thud on glass,
each hair hollow and clear,
though everyone sees
a bear white as a towel
thrown in.

MARYBETH HOLLEMAN

## Dispatch from Siberia

They live and work along the northern edge of land
where ice touches down every fall, later and later now,
and not as far south, so that walrus—tens of thousands
of long-toothed soft brown bodies—have immigrated
farther north and now gather just outside
their towns, beach en masse and wait for the ice
which is later and later, so that these men,
with their wide stances and wider smiles, armed with nothing
but sticks and the sense that generations of northern living
have given them, pray to their spirits and protect those walrus,
at first from polar bears, moving in waves along the coast,
roaming wide in search of food, following scent of walrus
and then carried out on that ice, staying with ice as it
recedes so far that they have not come back, those bears,
to this shore, and are either drowned or starved or moved
to other shores, Canada or Greenland, where ice still stays near,
and now from curious townspeople and foreign tourists,
circling near and clicking cameras and causing stampedes
in which thousands, pups and their mothers, are trampled
to death, so these brave men, armed with nothing
but sticks and a belief in the world they inhabit, carry
the carcasses far from town, leave them to feed
passing polar bears, and the first year, over one hundred bears
came and ate every morsel, but since then, with the ice
carrying the bears away, the mound of carcasses remains
rotting on the tundra, on this northern shore
where these men, smiles as wide as ever, continue to believe.

# How to Grieve a Glacier

It's not something you can hold in your arms.
You can't rock with its image in a blanket
and keen away the nearing pain.

That white face is distant, and cold, unrelenting
in its forward grind to the sea,
stalwart even as it thins, crumbles, pulls back
into history and oblivion.

The sun itself finds nothing to love,
save soft rivulets of water its rays release
from eons of hard frozen luck.

But I tell you I do love this blue-white giant,
and grieve its leaving, even as I thrill to watch
thunderbolts of ice crash into azure seas.

So we sit, you and I, scanning the newly revealed
and imagining what next will show itself,
what balded rock and bared shoreline,
as ice slips and pulls away in great chunks.

We know it is leaving, abandoning us
to what our kind has created,
and we know its gift of rarified water
will only bring more sorrow.

Yet it is a gorgeous deterioration.
Glowing face of one turned toward
what the living cannot see.

# Wing Feather

I swore to take only pictures and leave only footprints, but I cannot leave a single one of the plastic bottles on the beaches. My parents make their living by bottled water, leaving me to shoulder that weight every time a bottle washes to shore, half-full of water not as pure as what these streams give. I gather them, stuff them into crevasses in my kayak holds, a full empty load. On this last evening's beach, no different: I pick up both bottles, empty and crush them, take one more step and find an eagle feather, so perfect I look up to see if its owner still soars above. An immature bald eagle, by the mottled white and brown, and so large it must be a wing feather. Thinking it my reward for cleaning the beach, I thank the bird and pick it up. But it's not long before the burden of ownership sets in, and I wonder: was it a gift to be taken, or a gift to be seen and left? If I take it, I promise to return it within the year, after gleaning the muse from its vanes. Sitting on my desk, something might change: perhaps a thin layer of dust, or the dry air, or the smooth surface of a desk instead of the wet, cobbled beach. Too late I will realize it was never the feather I wanted, but that moment on the beach: living like that, being like that.

# JOYCE SUTPHEN

## Chickadees

The winter we got the new windows,
with their adjustable disappearing
shades, I spent hours watching

the chickadees catapult themselves
in and out of the bushes
on the other side of the glass.

As always, it was a cold winter,
but the chickadees knew how to
adapt. They remembered

where they had hidden every seed,
and like winter bees, they knew
how to dream of summer.

Later, I saw them, resurrected
and glorious in the branches
of the burning bush—resplendent

in their down-layered jackets,
each one impeccably capped—
little bellhops in the Sky-Blue Hotel.

## Amelia Earhart, Rock Springs 1931

We're trying to leave the hotel, but keep forgetting
things back up in the room: sunglasses, paper cup
full of coffee, wallet. I make multiple trips
from car to second story. The carpet is the same
in every hallway until I lose track of which floor
I'm on. I have to force myself to pay attention.
The car is running under the front awning.
The one insistence that we are somewhere specific
are the photographs in the halls: coal miners
below ground in 1928, an 1950s oil derrick
in "unknown location." Next to the check-in desk,
a framed photograph of Amelia Earhart
in a Rock Springs hangar where she'd stopped
to refuel. She's in front of her plane, smiling,
surrounded by locals who have turned out to see her.
One boy leans too far into the picture. It seems important
to remember this: her fabulous jumpsuit, the way
the propellers stretch out above her as if offering
some kind of shelter. When we finally leave,
we drive through blank desert country, tossing
our orange peels onto the car floor. We'll clean them
later. This feels like Western expanse. Stretches
of dirt, rock, sagebrush but punctuated by
pipeline stations and natural gas wells. Billboard:
*the most important thing to come out of our mines*
*is the miners.* They've tapped out on coal,

have moved onto trona, used as toothpaste filler
or to condition water or to clean the flesh
off trophy skulls. We probably have some
in our suitcases. Instead of town names, the exit signs
advertise chemical plants: Solvay, Tronox.
The names have changed since I last drove through.
We can't see it, but massive networks of mines
stretch beneath us. I'm already unable to recall
details of the hotel. We're driving toward a pile
of mist. I have trouble staying awake on this stretch.
In the past I've pulled over at abandoned gas stations
or firework stands to nap when scanning the radio
for station blips wore out. We're talking now
about my widowed sister, whom we agree
needs to move back home now. She's still
living near the facility where her husband worked,
where they manufacture rocket motors,
where they store and treat hazardous waste. Wait,
that gorgeous white cloud on the horizon
is actually the Jim Bridger Plant. 37 deaths
attributed annually to its fine particulate pollution.
It's called the Green River formation,
but everything here is brown, even the Dog Park
at Little America, which is just a gated plot
of dirt and concrete. My sister says she's afraid
she'll forget her husband's face if she leaves

their house. That's what photographs are for,
my husband says. But it's not the same, it's like
cheating to need something to hold. To have
to have a marker. We drive past the turnoff
for the fossil beds on cruise control. No one's sure
what caused the tumor. I scan the sky where
jet planes leave contrail messages I can't read.
A fraction of his cremains were launched into the air.
A crowd gathered. My sister was there to mark
the occasion and then that ceremony was over.
Ways we disappear into an expanse: clouds
look like islands and bodies become a cloud.
Magpies and crows congregate on smears
of roadkill every few miles. At first
I slow down when I spy each dark mass.
But if we're ever going make it home, I just
have to trust their wings will stretch and
lift off, that they'll scatter into the sky.

# Fruits of Our Labor

Health officials found a coyote carcass
in the freezer at the local buffet.
Worse: everyone seems relieved
it was not a dog. How can I still crave
a bowl of that golden soup? I should
be careful with what I carry. My belly, huge
and helpless, demands that every car stop
at crosswalks and every door be opened
for me. I rinse and rinse each berry
in my breakfast bowl, delivered to me
by men who walk in biohazard suits
through the strawberry rows. When passing by
the industrial-scale orchard, I do not
breathe in too deeply: those flawless
blooms, their pesticide coats. What kind
of bird still nests in those trees? What
kind of hatchling? I'd advise them
to keep on flying but what tree or field
is left to make into a home? After dinner,

I find myself walking through the wrong door
into the restaurant kitchen and wish
the workers in their hairnets would tell me
their opinion about which fancy stroller
I should buy. They have other
concerns. Their faces are masked
by scalding dishwasher steam. My plate
was so clean. I have a feeling all sorts
of things are kept back here, and
I have never seen. When the pains
begin to seize my belly, I breathe in deeply
over and over and remind myself
*I am a flower waiting to unfold.*
I am handled very carefully
by men wearing gloves. I am worried
they won't be safe enough.

## list of vanishing species

the restaurant walls were patinaed    the paint peeling    but the chandelier was there to
reassure us it was on purpose    *squid ink brioche*    *sea urchin pate*    we were seated
by the window but it was already dark    only one street light on this block right off the
tourist grid we'd walked    trying to consult a map which displayed notable Victorian

architecture    the world's first steam-powered clock    attractive people scurried through
steady rain in costume    wonder woman    caveman in rubber flipflops    a passel of
slinky cats of which my husband approved    I watched two people hurry to spread tarps
over something in the underpass    their movements so professional I thought they were

street vendors    until I caught a glimpse of dirty plush animals underneath    still I
I needed it explained to me    that these were necessities    mounded there    at the
restaurant we kept misunderstanding the punny menu    *Boar'n Ultimatum*    *Crouching*
*Tiger Hidden Leek*    we chewed octopus    savored duck confit    we could not tell the

fat from meat    earlier we'd watched humpbacks slip above the water and then back beneath

from the middle of the boat so I wouldn't get sick    my husband said hotel turn-down service

was ridiculous    but I loved that the rose-scented bath salts were always replenished

loved the invisible hand that tuned in light jazz on a channel I could not find myself    once

we walked in on the maid lining up our slippers by the bed    and we all apologized but for

what    we couldn't see the whales' whole bodies    just dorsal fin and fluke    I had

fantasized they would avail themselves to me    but long after they vanished the scent of

rotten fish drifted to our boat    at the restaurant a man walked in    something on his

shoulder wrapped in a garbage bag    I didn't understand at first    it was part of his

costume that he forgot to unveil once sheltered from the rain    a stuffed parrot maybe?

we searched him for context    mullet wig    piratical jacket    maybe a monkey under

there?    he was meeting a woman at the bar    her architectural hair roped in tiny

Christmas lights       and topped with a lit-up star       I swiped back through the photos I'd

earlier clicked       dark slick shapes humping up from water       our tour guide had held up       but they

charts of different species       on the menu we suspected other items were jokes

were just food we didn't know       *byssop and cardoon*       we talked about the news


*coronation grapes*       how scientists said a new age of extinction was underway       the

world's species half gone       via climate or harpoon       our tour guide knew the whales from

the scars that crisscossed their backs       souvenirs of passing ships       at the bar the woman's

star was blinking       with each drink the man was getting louder       we thought maybe we


could see at last a second head shrouded on his shoulder       it was hard to look

away       in the restaurant window of course we saw ourselves       and beyond that an

expanse of park so dark we could have been looking into the sea       the lights had all been

broken on purpose       to cover a part of the city that didn't want to be seen       pedestrians

stumbled past      some drunk because it was Halloween      and others just fucked up
a jittery woman outside sang loudly to herself      she didn't know she was performing but
we could hear a little of her song      the rain made a different sound when we left the
restaurant      pattering on the homeless tents that had risen in the dark      the next morning

sunlight streamed into the hotel lobby when we were checking out      women in wedding
dresses had draped themselves over the sleek furniture      a photo shoot      they were so
composed we could tell they weren't really brides      later we might discover them again in
some glossy magazine      like artifacts of some vanished life      back home we saw

the photographs      read online about the whale washed up by the terminal bay      its entire
body on display      rostrum      ventral grooves      phalangic bump and fluke      it was
unclear the cause of death      and ferry service kept running regularly      shuffling
people from shore to shore      the ships unzipping the water in their wake

## Seascape with Evacuating Animals

all of the ocean creatures
have been ripped out
of the pop-up book        no one's

actually been using the trashcan
lately        just tossing used
kleenex        strands of

dental floss in its general
direction        I have been stepping
over a grinning paper shark

on the bathroom carpet
for a week now        I suspect
my missing car keys

number among this
flotsam        it is fall and spiders
are seeking sanctuary

from the cold        are squeezing
their plump bodies
under door cracks

every morning
I wash one down the drain
a new one dangling

over my head        I shower
praying steam doesn't slicken
whatever informs its

tenuous hold     I feel I
should announce now
it is not ideal to have

carpet near a toilet     eventually
everything floats down
to clogged waterways

where by mistake birds
and fish fill their mouths
with plastic bags     chemical

foam     I can think of
nothing to do with this
limp book but return it

to the shelf     an empty ocean
how many times have I
held two things in my hands

and thrown the wrong one away

# THOMAS R. SMITH

## For the Turtles, and Us

In marshy sloughs beneath the upper dam,
turtles sun on half-submerged tree-trunks.
It's early April, and warm enough
to stir in us ambivalent enjoyment—
we like the weather but worry about the climate.

If we're still, the turtles remain
badged darkly on dark branches, their shells
the dull burnish of antique coins
or the worn polish of old soldiers' helmets
unearthed from a forgotten battlefield.

How sensitive they are to any sudden
motion of ours. Yet they cohabit
peacefully with a pair of nesting
Canada geese in their calm backwater
ringed with cattails and soon-to-leaf willows.

How stagnant, already, their tiny inlet,
scummy with pea-soup green, possibly
grown from the same toxic phosphorous
fertilizer runoff from yards and fields
making dead zones in the Mississippi.

Dead zones in us too? Who will change it
if not us? And how long can the turtles,
so practically armored by nature, whose heads
dimple the filmy water when they duck
our scrutiny, keep soldiering on?

## Oklahoma, 2017

In early March, hundreds of square miles
in Oklahoma are burning. 'Never
seen anything like it,' says one official.
Last year's rains produced a bumper grass crop
now tinder in this year's drought. Oklahoma,
home state of Trump's EPA head, Scott Pruitt,
climate change denier, brazenly
beholden to fossil fuel interests.
Roll back protections of air and water
and get out of the way of big oil and coal!
Forget the hardness of Flint, the hatefulness
of Love Canal. Put gag orders on scientists,
scrub inconvenient language from websites.
One coordinated attack after another
on the wellsprings of public health and the planet's.
We understand short-term plunder for the rich,
but what's in it for the rest? These tear-downs
must be defiant validation for
those who hate others more than they love
themselves, sufficient to satisfy them
that their will is being done as they're prodded
down the chute to the loading cattle truck.

## Zebra Mussel

No larger than a pea,
this miniature shell affixed
to the stone I pick from Cass Lake.
Back from the center seam
fine lines of brown and green curve
on a handsome blue-eyed blue.
I believe you want to live,
so far as a creature so elementary can,
and I don't blame you for the damage
you do, in terrible innocence,
to our northern waters. I believe
that inside your tiny closed helmet,
razor-sharp to the feet of unwary swimmers,
you also keep a grain of God.
But where you sow your profligate seed,
other lives, of fish and of plants,
fade as though you were a bag of poison
dumped from a boat. You sprout
on every small, wave-washed stone
I examine on this lake's life-
cleansed shoreline, a morbid, sterilizing
beauty. My heart becomes a wet stone
sinking in dismay at how one
so small can desolate its world.

ANNE HAVEN McDONNELL

## The Underworld Is Alive

*After a talk by Sandra Steingraber*

she said, and I mean *alive*. We drill through 400 million orbits of earth to sea lilies and squid that bloom like black ghosts, and we kill to get there. Of course, life sleeps in earth's heavy body. Of course the seams of life are seamless. Of course we have forgotten our hunger. Our water bodies tilt, our tides wash through, salty blood seeks sea. We have not forgotten our hunger. *We are the adults now,* she says to my sleeping hands, the fish who quicken in my body's rivers, the roads outside press against the giant warm turning of earth. One in four, three, two mammals will be gone—their furred bodies, nipples, warm breath gathering in the corners. A tawny flank, an ear, a wet black eye. I think of the seals who watched us, bald heads bobbing in the waves, the dark pools of their eyes following our every move. *We were wrong about the underworld,* we knew it would be this way—the waters gone from the leaves, the tongues, rains, tears. Not wasted, but taken.

## Once There Were Fish

Once, the rivers moved both ways, up
    through the one mind of salmon, silvered
into many bodies, sweeping across
    the land like weather. I stood
knee-deep in the last of it, Alaska
    the year the tundra burned,
the year the old ones fell through
    the ice that always held. I saw
an old buck, hook-jawed and mottled,
    sloughing off skin, nosing his weary
way past my shin. Then I saw the river
    turn back its silted face, mumbling
to its darling gravel along the shore.
    The gulls lifted and flung
their white flags, their shrieks tearing
    holes in the rain. I tell you
I saw it as it once was here
    and everywhere—the ground
thundering thousands of hooves,
    wings darking out
the sky, numberless animals
    spreading and gathering like storms.

How salmon carried the sea's longing
    to return. I stood knee-deep
in my own longing, casting
    along the edge of current and slack,
dragging orange yarn tied on a hook
    across their path. And when
the sockeye struck, the yank
    pulled both the oldest
and youngest parts of me. And when
    I pressed my palm on the flank,
that golden eye—cold
    and steady as it stared
where? Shelves of ice sluffing
    into sea, rivers running straight
down the moulins. The rushing
    world, the melt. The fire.
The fish shuddering still
    under my hand.

## the woman who married a bear

I've never seen a bear bared
to air, skinned to a pearled
blue—the color of inside
shells or secrets. I've heard
hunters shudder—how human
they look, hung there upright.
It reminds me of the bear who roamed
New Jersey with mangled feet,
lumbering on hind legs like a person
in fur, holding those poor
paws to his chest. Bipedal,
fans called him Pedals, and cried
when the hunter shot him.
All the ways a distance
can collapse or be crossed.
Everyone wants to see a bear,
warm and alive and running
away, like I saw one,
her rounded heavy rear,
pelt rippling as she plowed
uphill, putting the earth
between us. Her body dark
and round like the hole underground
where she curled, suspended, gathering
the braided medicines of sleep
and earth. In the old stories,
people who cross over never
quite return. Once I dreamed
my body was enveloped
by warm dark fur. It wasn't a symbol
of you, or him, or the love I always
wanted from her—it was new—
dank breath and cool seeps
in the cave, wrapped by that
bear as if sleep there could carry
me back where I belong.

# Check Dam

It's not lost on me: white woman
with my students—Hopi, Dine, Apache, Menominee—
when we form a line, passing rocks
hand to hand, building little check dams
above the head cut where rain, when it comes,
comes hard and fast, carving this dusty soil,
grazed and razed and taking hold
in the low places where water slows,
sinks and becomes that yellow blanket:
cow-pen daisies and four-o-clocks,
purple aster and thyme-leaf spurge, the juniper
shading tiny gardens where the pinion
are coming back. Carl throws some seeds
of blue grama and buffalo grass, while Michael
scatters Apache cotton seeds his grandfather gave him.
The tips of grama grass are curved and lit
like commas in the sharp fall light.

Once, this whole place was gardens—
check dams and rock mulch for fields of corn,
squash, beans, cotton, and whatever else
the People grew here. Now these empty
houses stretch for miles, too quiet
with their driveways, newly planted trees,
and gravel yards. Water maps its own
time across the desert, carves
earth into a canyon growing
beneath the barbed wire border
of our campus. Still, here we are, tossing seeds
above a rock pile, trying to slow the rain.

# GREG NICHOLL

## Wildfires

A fraction of an ember is all it takes.
                Acres of grass dry as tinder.
        Across the prairie, roofs

are doused with water to hinder
                the burn. Still, they are just
        kindling awaiting flames.

Campfires. Matches. Bottle rockets.
                A spark pitched
        from a train wheel as it strikes the metal rail.

In Pennsylvania, a town has been burning
                since 1962.
        It started at the local dump. No one

wanted piles of garbage that close to the cemetery,
                so they set it on fire.
        That year a lone cinder

bore through the cement barrier.
                Now each year the fire
        spreads, shoots through veins of coal,

mine shafts beneath the town converted
            into a furnace
        that burns hotter than the surface of Mercury.

Roads melt from beneath. Sinkholes emerge
            without warning.
        Back West, a rat climbs into an attic,

chews through the sheathed wiring.
            A single spark
        to start the fire. The trucks

seen moving along the highway
            long before
        their sirens were ever heard,

the embers already cooling
        · on the ground
        where children now gathered to play.

# Drought

Suddenly hundreds of gulls
descend the steppe, upset

our notion of where we belong.
Wharfs. Canneries.

The deck of a fishing boat
docked at Bodega Bay.

We might even accept Vegas
with its artificial lakes.

Not Wyoming where sun
hardens the earth and heads turn

toward the horizon at the slightest
suggestion of a storm.

The clay beneath these lawns
too dense to hold moisture,

or frankly, unwilling.
On coastal beaches the ground

is less sure of itself, shifts
with the tide, drags an entire

resort into the sea. No one was there
to watch it fall.

Where once stood a natatorium,
post office, hotel, now yields

to dunes and the occasional seagull
plucking at the remnants

of a rain-sodden crab. That
gull makes sense, belongs

to that seaside cliff, not like
these imposters who touch down,

sniff at what little trash they can find,
then scatter as quickly as they arrive.

## Miriam Bird Greenberg

## A Hermeneutics of Fire

When fires burned on the mountain all season
I kept below,
  and did what I could:
  I placed dishes of water at the perimeter of my yard for the foxes;

I collected juniper berries;
rusted kettles;
  the leaves of trees I feared I wouldn't see again;
  and feathers. I kept a church-key

for unspooling film from its spiral and walked long distances
into the char, heat
  rising from the earth,
  to take pictures which unveiled their dark edges behind the fog

in their bath. The birds had gone, and I kept asking
for rain
  but beneath the eaves of my cabin heat refused
  to give way. Fire jumpers spilt from their parachutes

into the flames, and I told myself, what is belief, anyway,
but the pattern of smoke
  on a low ceiling where, below, a candle
  has burnt every night

for years. Fire moves slowly,

and with ravenous care,
as in flickering films of the Hindenburg spilling open onto the air,
the cool, muscular coil

of a snake shrugging off its scales in the rafters. Every morning

I walked home from the forest
of heat, its houses hollowed to beams in the burn, and asked myself
What is belief but the pattern of smoke,

a brief pleasure? Swallows, when they'd gone, spilt from their bearded nests

into the low dusk

moving, unshadowed,
into what is known.

# MICHELLE ACKER

## Hurricane Florence, September 2018

*Roanoke, VA*

Ex-Floridian, I thought I'd left them behind, but
there's nothing on Earth that doesn't puddle
everywhere you walk. When I was young

I begged for hurricanes, pleaded, prayed
to whatever god or king casts violent eyes
like dice into the ocean. "Instead of snow

days," we joked, "we get hurricane days."
It was exciting to hide, darkly
pretending at disaster though, every time,

my own fridge stayed cold
and my tapwater clean. At that age, I liked
the idea that I understood certain

insistencies: one gallon per person per day
of bottled water. How to hand-crank a radio.
The way a hurricane's leading and lingering clouds

thread across the windless sky, pushed
by pressure. When I was thirteen, a storm
snuffed out the school's power, so we massed

in the gym, in the dim light, charged
with the water rising inside us that licked
at every weak seam. Coach

opened windows to relieve the heat,
though through them the storm spat fat splatters
on the bleachers. A bird flew in,

and for hours it sheltered, ruffled, hunched
as far from the sweating mob of middle-schoolers
as it could get. I watched it like a cat

watches a raven, or an albatross: hungry
and outmatched. They dismissed us from the gym
at the end of the day; cancelled school the next.

Back then, I loved how the rain ran trenches
out by my house, how all our tall pines
bowed though elsewhere, people were

drowning. The puddles shine like footprints
welled with mercury. I can't help it:
homesick, I still hope for rain.

# Elizabeth Bradfield

## Permeable

*After Leah Wong, from Cape Cod*


           Below us: water (fresh lens).  And
      below that: a different water
(salt soused).  This youngest end
     of a glacier-spat spit,
        this outwash plain,
grains permeable, percolating,


        angular, rough, tilted
     piled & drifted into
        dunes, swales.  Space
     between the planes.  Slip and seep.

How does it hold?  How are
     we held?  As we bustle, as we duck
        whatever current licks
    at us.  A comfort to river


        my own salt through a pond
     which is an open eye of the water
body (aquifer) a well sucks
     from under backyard sand
        (pull too deep & you'll
    draw salt).  We float, placid,

though not untouched by what falls,
       heavy, from seeming-clear sky into
              nymph-body, fish-body.  Or what
       fins up from salt-depth, toothed.  Or
riptides (diver lost this summer
       & the body held two days
              before washed ashore).  Sorrow,

       I have felt you, seeping
              as the pond's larger body seeps,
       flows slow, finally rivers out
a few feet below mean high into larger
       water—you've seen those small rivers,
underworld-cool, veinlike and branching
       into our porous, dangerous world.

## KATHRYN SAVAGE

# Ophelia

When my son was learning
to speak

we watched local news. A red-gray
hurricane moved across the television. "Ophelia," I said.

"Baby," he said,
staring at the swirl.

The television looked like an ultrasound, or
the cosmos, or

an MRI brain scan. Stars over a great lake.

Ophelia had killed two men
and a woman in Ireland,

caused a red dust sun in London.

We watched her surge.

My son was young enough to remember
being water and then being

pulled from all he knew.

So I asked him again,
"Where's the baby?"

He walked to the screen,
touched the television's blood light.

# CINTIA SANTANA

## Grief, February

a warm one, though my friend tells me that in this state
we say this every year. No, I say, this one is different,
this one is warmer; it hasn't rained in weeks. The calving
of glaciers is not peaceful; it is *loud*. And I cannot stand
those shots of polar bears stranded on thin floats of ice:
the lone emaciated male now forced to swim, the Heligimbal
panning out, revealing—only then—the vast sea around him;
no ship will save him, his tide is *out*. And although they don't
show it, I can see it all—that's what the movie wants—we know
enough by now to contemplate the many ways of dying; why
watch just one? The hunger driving the bear out of his mind;
his inability to find firm footing; his tiring that turns to panic,
then back to tiring, but more so. All I can do then is hope
for his numbing, for sleep to overtake him before the water
ushers its ache into his lungs. That last time at the hospital,
the call was mine to make: my mother *on retreat*, my uncle-doctor
on the other side of the country talking me through it on the cell.
*Yes I said yes I will yes;* I was without ballast, I was without hull.
And I don't care what they say, that film crew is complicit,
abandoning the dying polar bear *so as not to fuck with nature*
—we make *posters* out of it, call it art, hawk it at suburban fairs.
It makes me want to can my grief like a tin of tuna, sell it in threes
—*I wore his coat for weeks.*

## Apocryphon of Ice

upon a time
        the ice advanced
  inexorably
          the trees
    retreated
       southmost

             step by
                glacial lobe receded
            downslope
                  ice tongue
            end moraine

                    in a land without trees
                  build with bone
                        my hand in the dark
                 thigh-high snow
                         skin boat, quiet

            my hand in the dark
                thigh-high snow
         swing saw
    bade me

        ice trade       bade me
        ice market     bade me
  gale-torn

pack ice
when the bush plane came
ice fog

*oil* the man said
*leasing*
wore
brand new
*more, too*
*aching*
*to be drilled*

pipeline followed the road
floating city
horizon
awake at night
heat-joy in my bones

*upin'ngakhaq*
skim, newly formed
crack
between earth and

fluted by meltwater
I forded
to pilot our boat

floe edge
ceiling of ice, split
sun lit the sea

ice cellar
filled with water

wintering grounds still
    snow-streaked

                            veins, blue-bleeding
                                fanned toward the sea

           shore-fast ice
                             breaks mottled
                                  open stretch

a road of water over
    ringed the island
                                 darkness

                  polar

                        pull of the sun
                                calved

ice sheets
  shelf ice
  sea ice
      buckled
                 drift ice

                        anchor ice
                          bottom-fast

                  ice famine

        rose

float

snowmobile
breakaway
slab
in need of

my hand in the dark

hand
dark
heat

joy in my
bones

drift

dream

*when the first snow fell*
*it fell for you*

# Hum

Slip of
bird
with fan
of furious
wings in
blossom's
throat I hear
your wing
-beat sing.
To nectar
you need
no key,
mid-rib
of leaf or
sip from
little red
vials
constantly
defiled;
starvation
staved
for one
more day.
Butterfly
weed, too,
bids your
wing
-whistle
come:
*sing me,*
*guard me,*
*lap me*
*with your*
*split*
*tongue.*

# Ode to Your Salmon Soul

to your mother and your father / and their mothers
and their fathers / to the pale pink of their love / and
their cold / unseasoned waters / because it made / you
you / you / Ode to your mouth gasping / to its echo
of my gasping / to your bludgeoning / which is my
bludgeoning / and the tears lost to this water / Ode
to the bear's maw / wound-wide and lovely-dark /
To the quiver and muscle / the barb / the tidal marsh
and the cruelty of shallows / To the fight / the current /
the heave and the climb / to the higher / higher / heights
and the estuary's sky / a riot of stars / silent winks
that bind / Ode to the slope / the steepness / the leap
and the lope / To the feast and the / stones / to Chinook
and Chum / To the / sweet / eelgrass to / the first gravel
nest / and the next / To your / rings / narrow / wide /
to your hump / your growing / teeth and your / kype
Ode to your / cherry / skin your darker / silver / blues
to your / milt your / red roe / spilling / ripe / Ode to you
to / you to / you / to the / river rumoring / home

# CRAIG SANTOS PEREZ

## Echolocation

*for "J35, Tahlequah"*

My wife plays
with our daughter
while I cook dinner.
On the news,
we watch
you struggle
to balance
dead calf on
your rostrum.

Days pass.
We drive
our daughter
to preschool and
to the hospital
for vaccinations.
You carry your
child's decom-
posing body
a thousand
nautical miles
until every wave
is an elegy,
until our planet
is an open casket.

How do you say,
"sorry," in your
dialect of sonar,
calls, and whistles?
What is mourning
but our shared
echolocation?

Today, you let go
so her body
could fall and
feed others.
Somehow,
you keep
swimming.
We walk
to the beach
so our daughter
can build sandcastles.
May she grow
in the wake
of your resilience.
May we always
remember:

love is our wildest
oceanic instinct.

# Thirteen Ways of Looking at a Glacier

*~recycling Wallace Stevens*

### XIII

Among starving polar bears,
the only moving thing
was the edge of a glacier.

### XII

We are of one ecology
like a planet
in which there were once 200,000 glaciers.

### XI

The glacier absorbs greenhouse gas.
We are a large part of the biosphere.

### X

Humans and animals
are kin.
Humans and animals and glaciers
are kin.

## IX

We do not know which to fear more,
the terror of change
or the terror of uncertainty,
the glacier calving
or just after.

## VIII

Icebergs fill the vast Ocean
with titanic wrecks.
The mass of the glacier
disappears, to and fro.
The threat
hidden in the crevasse
an irreversible clause.

## VII

O vulnerable humans,
why do you engineer sea walls?
Do you not see how the glacier
already floods the streets
of the cities around you?

## VI

I know king tides,
and lurid, unprecedented storms;
but I know, too,
that the glacier is involved
in what I know.

V

When the glacial terminus broke,
it marked the beginning
of one of many waves.


IV

At the rumble of a glacier
losing its equilibrium,
every tourist in the new Arctic
chased ice quickly.


III

Shell explored the poles
for offshore drilling.
Once, we blocked them,
in that we understood
the risk of an oil spill
to a glacier.


II

The sea is rising.
The glacier must be retreating.


I

It was summer all winter.
It was melting
and it was going to melt.
The last glacier fits
in our warm hands.

JAYNE FENTON KEANE

# 70 km Nth of Punta Arenas, Penguin Sanctuary, Otway Sound, Patagonia

Magellan's Penguins arrange their spines to match local boulders. Settler's grass appears as a whisper spelled in a flame as it roils around them. A body can mirror a stone when there is nowhere left to run. Driftwood and bone share histories of holding things upright. There's a 2,000 pesos admission price. Half-feathered downy chicks bigger than their mother slip on rocks smooth as new skin and white as plastic bags. The sea is a choppy emerald regurgitating skeletons and feathers as a fox pisses on his borders. The walking circuit is a trail of one foot in front of the other as the path appears and disappears in sericeous mist. Hares bolt in front of cars and parrots scatter from bushes in the distance. A condor hovers in a mirage of air currents as the feather in my pocket twitches with strange divinations. Stop here beneath this mountain, let its shadows embrace you like a pair of silken gloves. Even our milk began to spill in the pattern of a broken heart towards the end. I want to speak to you but my language bears only wild covenants. Incomprehensible, these topographies of chilled windy places in pre-storm light. I don't understand no entiendo no entiendo such are the odes. Smile even though you don't understand. Take fir branch and animal bone and snap. Step and climb, pull and pick, step and climb, pull and pick. Here's a good spot for a photograph.

# SARA RYAN

## From the Window

what I'm telling you is all truth. I don't know why you'd think I'd lie to you. next door, bells are ringing a sad song. I can hear the muffled metal through the walls. my dear, listen: the snow is falling in sheets of milk. California is on fire. the horses are burning in pairs. in dozens. the blazes stop at the ocean and spit at the water. and what about that storm—it swallowed two people into its belly. that cold, dark lake. the trees on the ridge splintered like toothpicks. the power lines brought down like spools of yarn. that man, with a small girl in his mouth. all the men, their cheeks puffed out—bulging with milk and hair. those dreams I had as a child. my strong and clicking knees, how they once could run for miles and knew how to best carry me. when I think of the word power, I think of electricity. a spark. fire churning through national parks at hundreds of miles an hour. I've given up on taking photographs from airplane windows. nothing looks as impressive on camera. the world lets me down this way. all the time.

## She Has a Pair of Simple Eyes

in the end,
one snake always wins.
she is long
and dense

with muscle.
her jaw
a milky wetness—
unhinged.

of all her
possible truths,
one slithers
through—it is
a poison, hot sounds
of metal strings.

no matter what,
the clever lady snake
ends up with the rest.
in the yellow
plastic drum,

choking on scales
and venom.
rattles shiver
like bleak castanets.

bleached white
by sun. in the end,
dunked
in the fryer oil.

or coiled tight
and slow
from cold. she's skin
and diamonds.

broken fanged queen.
she remembers
what has happened to her.
she has drawn
slim and long
lines in the sand.
her bones
are thin and pliable—
an atlas
of spine and rib.

she sheds
and swallows whole.
she strangles. suffocates.
how strong

she is. even as she is broken
apart by children
and men, her nerves
writhe in protest.

somehow, still,
she is a chorus
of tongues pushing
against the backs
of teeth.

imagine
that power. imagine
curling around
something and claiming it
yours. imagine
owning

an entire sound.
in the end, one snake
spirals and survives
and keeps
on living.
in that desert valley,

between canyons
of oil and cotton.
she sheds her skin
and vibrates. she is living.
fighting. she is ready
to strike.

# AMY MILLER

## Cougar Spotted behind Rooster's Restaurant

Everyone jokes he came for the chicken but of course
it's the rats and the squirrels and maybe an errant pet.
And the looming green stockroom of the dumpster.
And the mountain to the south with its hundred days
of snow. And the mountain to the east hidden
by another mountain. And the hill the kids call a mountain
when they huff up the trail on a field trip heavy with flowers.
And the golf course and the pets eternal rest cemetery
and the Angus beef ranch and the rolling road
we drive between them, hills so dark green we call this not
South Medford, not Ireland, but Oreland. And really
only a practiced eye can tell the blurry body in the video,
long thick tail, little head, is even a lion. But our eyes
have seen them plenty on the signs along the trail—
*make yourself look large*—and the photos on Twitter
the tourists took a block outside downtown, huge cat
gliding past the windows. Everybody jokes it's all
because the deer are friendly, but really it's the springs
and their endless migration, the quail who shelter
in the blackberries everyone wants to shred, the hail
shotgunning summer's tomato crop. It's every
straight line we thought we drew. How the ground
is bending them even now.

# Wolf OR-7 Shares a Carcass with Coyotes

Uneasy. Torn. Contentious
brothers not brothers.
Who are we but stars
of our own wilderness?
There was baring and approach,
thrust, feign, a show
of who had the upper hand.
Then reversal. That taste—
something so long dead
and needles of hunger so hot
that I have to say
it was paradise, that mouthful
ripped in the presence
of who cares who,
their eyes hard on me
and waiting their turn.

# SARAH BROWN WEITZMAN

## A Well of Despair

A follow up to that classic
experiment done in the 60s

on young primates fed by wire
figures, how they always rushed

right after to snuggle
with some padded forms

though those never fed them
anything nor ever hugged them

back. What hunger
that softness satisfied

science wanted to know.
So now to have the facts

on this early lack of mother,
a modern steel-lined crib

for infant rhesus monkeys
without the former cotton

clutter, each in its own cylinder.
(The scientist had quite a bent

for lab language who named that place
"a well of despair.") Forty-five days

and forty-five nights of maternal
deprivation. While it lasts

each babe gives science its best
moments, watching through one-

way glass, persistent spindly arms

trying to cuddle the smooth steel
sides of those metal mothers.

# SUDASI CLEMENT

## B as in Bravo

After the bomb,
after the black rain falls
and drifts eastward,
a jellyfish bloom begins.

Not the bell-shaped
creatures of the sea,
but babies, born
without bones.

Muddled dollops,
cellophane-skinned,
and inside—blur
of brain, polyp heart.

Mothers hurry to bury
soft-bodied boys,
grape-cluster girls,
ashamed.

After the great mushroom
bursts above the sea,
after Bokonijien and
Aerokojlol are vaporized,

an inch of poison ash
sifts onto turquoise water,
palm fronds, the islanders'
hair.

We tell them they're safe,
remind them these tests
are for the good of all
mankind. Truth lies

in the flesh of bluefin,
breadfruit, coconut,
crab, the unborn,
the stillborn.

*Bravo was the code name for an H-bomb the U.S. detonated over the Bikini Atoll in
1954. Due to a miscalculation, the blast was 1,300 times more powerful than each of the
bombs dropped on Hiroshima and Nagasaki. Three islands were completely obliterated.
To this day, "jellyfish babies" continue to be born in Micronesia.*

# EILEEN WALSH DUNCAN

## Possum Mouth

Cruncher of bones. Devourer
of venomous snakes. Slurper of the spineless
who hide underground, puffy with juice.

Your alligator jaw is the first harbinger.
No-one suspects a waddler. No-one
expects death to arrive on knobby pink feet,
mincing a bit along sharp stones.
Nor would said feet be swollen
and hairless, replete with opposable thumbs.
Death, aged and arthritically inflamed, gone out sans slippers,
one more senseless mission.

Your pert teeth, your rolled tongue
loom over insect nests, and roadkill
that pocks our rivers of asphalt. You pick ticks
from the belly of this world, your own
marsupial pouch slightly agape,
folds visible as you go. May you preside
over all untimely ends,
and till the carrion with your velvet chin.

CONNIE WIENEKE

## After Totality

The coyotes have shoved the night
under the door and into my room,
bringing along the neighborhood

dogs and owls, earwigs and mice.
Perhaps they only meant to lure
them, the dogs, for sport and not

for the easy meal. These coyotes
don't have an easy job of it, people
shooting at them across the cut

grass, setting traps others walk into.
Somehow coyotes get themselves
blamed for what happens: missing

pets, exhausted sleep. How strange
they make us dream. It's a week
after totality. The half-hearted moon

disappears behind the nearest hills.
Coyotes talk about it most nights, not
the eclipse they stuck their noses into,

seeing it for a trick to make humans
human again, open-mouthed, the middle
of the day. No, they talk about how hard

they have to work to keep the air alive
at night, to nudge stranded stars back
on course with yips and closed eyes.

# JUAN J. MORALES

## My Eco-Crimes

Forgive me for running the tap too long,
houseplants murdered, paper towels
and paper plates, brand new light bulbs
dropped, the shabby pens lost,
and house lights left on when no one was home.
Sorry for the now-extinct mice
I killed for living in my air conditioner,
the flowers cut before they went to seed,
fruits and veggies I didn't get around to eating
or bottles and cans too lazy to fish
from the trash. I apologize for leaving
the crust of my bread, for pitching
tin foil after one use.

But I'm not sorry for
the smokes I smashed out after a few drags
during the countdown toward a polluted future.
I will miss the days of excessive living
with soap or washers and dryers or
radios or wallets or gas stations
from the salad days when I thought
recycling was good enough.

BENJAMIN GOLUBOFF

## Environmental Studies

We drive all night in two college vans,
west through Roundup-Ready corn and soy,
crossing at Council Bluffs into CAFO country.
The students don't seem to mind the long drive.
There is good signal on the interstate:
they Yikyak and Snapchat,
microblog and game.
At dawn, from a bridge over the Platte River,
we watch ten thousand cranes
rise screaming into a sunrise of blood.
The students are impressed;
they hold up their phones.

# KAREN SOLIE

## Four Factories

1.

At the nominal limits of Edmonton, refineries wreathed
in their emissions, huge and lit up as headquarters
or the lead planet in a system, as the past
with its machinery exposed—
filters, compressors, conveyors, you name it—
basement upon basement upon basement.
Around them gather opportune spinoffs, low-slung
by-product support outfits named in functional
shorthand. *Altec, Softcom, Norcan, Cancore,*
subsidiaries crawling onto the farmland.
Employees are legion, transient,
and union turning what happened before we existed
into something we can use, at capacity
day and night. As we sleep, they build our future.
Which, as the signs say, belongs to all of us, is now.


2.

Worth leaving the highway for. Gorgeous
at sunset, really outstanding,
the potato chip factory at the east end

of Taber, which is a kind of town.
It's painted a bright and not entirely baffling
turquoise, for who would want

their snacks to issue from a dour scene?
Crowding the parking lot's acre of slab,
against evening's mauves, pinks, blues

and tangerines, it looks like a monument
to grad night in the midwest
or a wedding after-party at the Holiday Inn.

There's a nicotine tinge to the white concoction
frothing from the stack. In the morning
it's work, an okay wage, metal door

of the employees' entrance ugly
and dented forever, yesterday's effluent
still fizzing in the drainage pool.

3.

The global appeal of concrete is not accidental.
Through it, our modern version is realized. That "cement"
and "concrete" are used interchangeably
is one of the most interesting things about it.
This confusion is rooted deeply in our language.
West of Dead Man's Flats, at Exshaw, they make
cement. Pre-eminent in the limestone gap, the plant
appears to describe its situation accurately, reflected
in the lake that cools the wastewater.
Scenery north of Heart Mountain goes vague
in kiln dust from the clickers.
Pity the diatoms, first to go, trout eggs
choked by sediment and gravelly streambeds,
ducks in chloride runoff. Pity us,
we're all messed up about it. Nearby are the old
company towns. Kananaskis and its lime plant.
Seebe's power dam has closed. But in concrete
is it ancient technology ushered into
the 21st-century: in condos, dude ranches,
four-season resorts, the demand for improved
infrastructure and amenities in the recreational
community of Lac des Arc.

4.

In the cold, the blood smell clings. In heat,
        flies observe it. A functional non-
architecture's slaughter capacity.
        *We're coming back to Newfoundland*

*with our mobile recruiting team!*
        No experience necessary. High school
not necessary. Must be willing
        to work with a razor-sharp knife. Revised

prison recruitment strategies. E. Coli.
        Recalls. Must tolerate extreme heat
and cold. Bandidos in town on the recruitment
        initiative. RAID. Burgeoning drug

trade. Brooks' Chamber of Commerce
        welcomes your input. Delusive, debilitating,
awe-inspiring tedium. *I Heart Alberta*
        *Beef.* Team members should expect

heavy physical labor and fast-paced
        repetitive tasks. Team members
should expect to be called team members.
        The killing floor. Caricatures of supervisory

misconduct. Unprecedented growth. Labour
        unrest. A crew of managerial thugs
mobilized from Arkansas. The Canadian
        Forces steps up to its recruitment

campaign. Our industry's future remains
        secure. Additional openings in rendering
and hides. Animals are not our friends. Sign
        on the highway, *Always, 100 Jobs!*

# HEIDI LYNN STAPLES

## The Manager

*Chem Waste; Emelle, Alabama—largest hazardous waste site in the U.S.*

What you have heard is not quite true. We were welcomed at the site. The PR person greeted us with a handshake, the guard waved us in. There were notebooks, posters about hierarchies of waste management, a conference table. He offered us water, soda, an analogy. It was everything you have on your kitchen sink, we have here. It was all the products we all enjoy. It was all you girls paint your nails, acetone. You all use Draino. Your clothes for example, where do you get the dye? Shoes, the adhesives. Drycleaners. What do you do with that by-product? Jewelry, everybody likes a nice ring and a watch. But there's going to be a by-product. Same thing with food. At large quantities, it's going to be hazardous. Walmart, Target, Lowes, tons of damaged goods. We take care of that. The worst was the Pierre Cardin. Week after week it kept coming, acrid sweet smell. Bad-run on cologne, head starts pounding. All of us took notes. Shooting-range bullets—lead bullets, excavate the bullets or there's going to be environmental damage. Particulate matter. We take care of that. What we have is a legacy issue. Stock-piles all over the world. Nerve-gas disposal. To be a world power, you have to have something defensible. You don't want to admit it. By truck and by rail. Flammable, poisonous, corrosives, liquids, sludges, solids. We asked if he ever saw anything like poetry. He leaned out of his seat, grabbed a bucket. Dinosaur poop, he said, passed the bucket around like a bread basket. We took our pieces, placed them on the table. They formed a tiny Stonehenge there. We find fossils, he said. This is inland prehistoric ocean. In the entry way, you'll see 13 Plesiosaurus vertebrae. I like going down there into the excavation site and finding the fossils. Never get any shark's teeth. The others do. Just last week, they found handfuls of them, and I was just out there. Right there in that spot. Me? Nothing. He looked down at his hands. And what of that fool's gold, that shit we'd arranged? Some sort of monument? Temple? What sacrificed? Remains inscrutable.

# Elise Hempel

## Progress at the Development

They're making the lake today at Lakewood Village,
the tractors and bulldozers roaring, cutting out
an instant shore, a rectangle ordered to fit
the perimeter of new houses and garages.

By noon, they clear the dust, unroll the huge
black hose to fill it in and promptly start
to plant the trees, all spaced three feet apart.
By five, they drop into place the little bridge.

Now those who left this morning to the scene
of a field will return tonight
to saplings standing in their silent rows,
a plane of blue instead of shifting green.
A bridge where no direction was, a straight
line of ducks replacing the scattered crows.

# DEBRA MARQUART

## 3. Frack

*from Small Buried Things*

first the bakken   then the three forks formation   even deeper
    the oil patch, they call it
        two miles below the surface

oil embedded in shale
late devonian   remnants of the anoxic sea   the coastal carbonite layer
deposited when the middlewest was inner ocean

four hundred billion barrels, estimated   rest there   perhaps more   light and tight
the largest oil find in north american history
    conflict-free oil, they say
    ending the dominance of energy-rich rogue nations

the boom began in montana, alberta
    then spread to north dakota
        drawn within our borders
            by a friendly change to the state tax code

now eleven thousand wells pump
    a million barrels a day
        thirty thousand new workers converging on small towns
        people housed in man camps
        mostly good people, some desperate, some dangerous

the talk is about the rise in crime—robberies, stabbings, domestic disputes
    a sidney woman, early morning jogger, mother and math teacher
    grabbed from the side of the road
    later found strangled

the murderers bought a shovel at walmart to bury her
    then returned it for a refund later
        that's how the police caught them

so, the talk centers on the observable
    the damage to infrastructure
    the eyesore roads where there were no roads before
    the old highways, pitted and full of potholes   undriveable   dangerous,
    the speed of the oil and water trucks on the public roads
    the rise in highway fatalities

to frack you must drill down
    through topsoil, stratum, sedimentary rock
       down through fresh water aquifers,
            to reach the dolomite   the source rock

drill vertically then horizontally to reach the shale
    injecting millions of gallons of water per frack
        laced with hundreds of chemicals (some of them linked to cancer)
            most of them proprietary to corporations
                unknowable to ordinary citizens

unaskable, since the halliburton loophole (of 2005)
    exempted fracking from protections guaranteed to all citizens
        in the safe water drinking act (of 1974)

we knew   we couldn't say   we didn't know

except what's certain—benzene, toluene, ethylbenzene, and xylene
    volatile organic compounds,
        and diesel fuel (around 1 percent per gallon) used on the bakken shale

plus, the radium inert in the rocks
brought back up in the fracking fluid
after it's made its long journey below to gather the oil
then brought topside to be separated out

and shipped to a wastewater center where it's *treated*   *cleaned*
    in condensate tanks, some of them lined, some unlined
        seeping into the ground, toxins evaporating into the air

what's left over, uncleanable
    trucked in water tankers to be disposed of    *reinjected*
        in the land previously known as away.

# SHARON SUZUKI-MARTINEZ

## Understanding Nessie

Once, there was a murky lake that roiled, it is said, due to the undulations of a monster. So scientists took two hundred-fifty DNA samples from Loch Ness to find answers in its biodiversity. They found the Loch Ness Monster could not be a dinosaur, dragon, whale, or shark, as previously believed. More likely, Nessie is "a gigantic eel, or just many small eels." Since childhood, I dreamt of an immortal Plesiosaur, but the possibility of a thousand small eels united as a superorganism wracked me with weird wonder. Superorganisms are individual animals or plants that have evolved to be interdependent rather than competitive. Think of ant colonies, beehives, and cults. Members are so buddy-buddy, an individual separated from its clique suffers an untimely death. Microscopic superorganisms have even been found with nanowires or tiny electrical bridges connecting each microbe. Perhaps in the future, people will be discovered to be so intimately nanowired. In the meantime, no one has actually found Nessie. Nevertheless, she swims through our collective imaginations, generation after generation, like unseen DNA lurking in our blood.

> We could be monsters
> made up of smaller monsters
> maybe vice versa.

## Satan Ruled Out as Experts Puzzle Over Mysterious Flaming Pit in Arkansas

*~headline*

*Well, that's Arkansas,* we sigh, putting down
the morning paper, our neighbor state
and thus a bit too close for comfort
metaphorically and otherwise, a hole
780 degrees by their measurements,
hot as hell we'd be tempted to say
if experts hadn't ruled that out—along with
thunderbolts from Zeus, presumably,
a crash-landed UFO, or merely
Mother Nature's barbecue (it's Arkansas).
And if instead of front-page news
I'd seen it in a dream, I'd think
like Yeats some revelation was at hand,
the Second Coming, surely,
or even just the First. But we know
what's been vexed to such a nightmare
heat, know not to scratch from the list
of suspects the drill and mine,
those deep veins crossed like swords
to spark the Ozark sky with pillars of flame,
pillars of smoke, the local faithful
still unconvinced it's not a sign
to turn from science and all such works
of man, the angels themselves
firing up what must come down.

# JULIA SPICHER KASDORF

## F-Word

*The industry spelling of fracking is actually fracing.*

Without the *k*, it looks less violent:
*water pressure creates fractures that allow*

*oil and gas to escape*—as if they
were trapped—*under tight regulatory control.*

Blame the fracktivists, fracademics. A bumper
sticker claims, *I'm surrounded by gasholes.*

*Frack her 'til she blows*, says the T-shirt stretched
over a roughneck's belly at the Williamsport Wegmans.

Frackville, PA, named for Daniel Frack, *vrack*,
from Middle Low German: greedy, stingy, damaged,

useless. *Are you going to say what the word suggests*,
a student timidly asks, . . . *to women, I mean?*

Fracket, a sophomore explains, is that hoodie
worn over a spaghetti-strap dress to a frat house,

an old jacket that won't matter if it gets stolen
or left behind on a flagstone patio, splattered

with someone else's vomit.

# Benjamín Naka-Hasebe Kingsley

## Nantucket Sleighride

*When you harpoon a whale, it bucks harder than a freight train off rails. It dives down deep as it can go, and takes your boat with it—fast—and that's the "sleigh ride": that last fighting gasp of leviathan through the sea.*
~ Browning Tyler, grandson of a Nantucket whaler, 81yrs old


You know the whale metaphor. You know all about
the beaten horse. Write this off as just another
dead animal poem. Or, dying, know that my people
weren't neatly arked by America two by two, white boys named
Noah harpooned our asses, by the tens by the thousands,
collared our necks with barbs and slugged lead
into our heads when we bucked, they dove in after
our oil and the good fat of our plains, from Sea to Shining
Sea. Now here we all are, a tangle of corpses
together we crabs in a clawed bucket list:
cross off every otherkind and colony—colonize
the crevice between my brown lungs, cremate me
in ashy anonymity before
I surface, I breathe, I war.

## Los Alamos, New Mexico: An Open Letter to Radiation Poisoning

It's 1943 & you're moaning your secret:
Manhattan Project. Ore, more accurately,
you're what our pickaxes tick-tick-scrape.
Shunting of our land, splintering Church Rock
& dethroning Crown Point. You're what
our native son's dig for: atomic #92.

It's 1945 & you're a rich tenor rising in fat men's
throats. You're the splintered soprano squealing
above Nippon sons, a hollow bullet served steamed
on "Silverplates," Boeing B-29 "Super-fortresses."
You're the loudest whistle whining above metropolitan
Japan. Where we hide beneath our desks. It doesn't
matter: you're so full of yourself since growing out
of nothing but the dry pustules shaved from our art-
eries, dug from the dirt of our burial mounded souls.
We built fire lines, then picked the petals off oleanders red
& pink: the first flower to bloom after your
kaboom at our scalded pink feet.

It's 2012 & you're *still* the abandoned Northeast Church
Rock mine. One of half a thousand permanent
waste sites oozing out of the Navajo Nation's
crippled left shoulder. You're not a secret
anymore, skittering down the runaway
veins of our once big men, our once little boys, the ones
with pickaxes who are like you now:
hollow & scraped & shunted
rising with atomic #redwhite&blue

It's 2000-fill-in-the-blank & you're the only voice
left to make sure aspens bloom again in our spring:
so our boys can pick up axes
silvery-grey, soft and strong, good for pulping
the paper our children use for finger painting
forests of strawberry blonde.

# KELLI RUSSELL AGODON

## SOS

In a country of too much everything
—too many orcas dying and chemical fires
creating radiant lightning, we wake to a morning
of mourning of what didn't live, a woman
stepping onto the train tracks and us,
a block away hearing the thud.
Sometimes we break the wishbone
without making a wish—my arm on your arm,
my head on your chest as if this will be
our silhouette forever, as if we're in charge
of our own disappearing.
Sometimes we want to cut ourselves
out of the world, but we laugh because
none of our knives are sharp enough
nor our dedication to leaving.
So tonight with the moon wilting, evening
overflowing into the canal where a nuclear sub
passes, guardians of what we can't see,
our reflections are employed by the waves
as if disaster was our business, as if we're not
wildly waving our distress flag
from the edge of this eroding shore.

## Beached Whale, Terrebonne Parish, 2016

Hard to imagine what drew the young
    bull sperm inland through Sister Lake

south of Dularge. No squid to chase toward the beach,
    no pod to follow into the cove, only shallow,

slow water and sand to hold its weight. I'd love
    to believe something in the line of trees along

the coast stoked    its primal heart. How golden
    it would be if the whale's old kin walked past

trees like ours into their first salt water. So much
    better to hold that dream than know the whale

swam in, dizzy from the water's heat, drunk
    on bacteria, or gobs of loose oil, unwilling to accept

the gift of open Gulf and long, deep breaths.

# STACEY BALKUN

## The Water, the Truth, the Water

*Used by Union Carbide during the active phase of plant operation, the chemical pond situated in the woods of Piscataway, NJ is located less than 500 feet from Wynnewood Swim Club.*

I go only as far as I dare                          a full-grown possum-girl

through the familiar neighborhood       past the NO TRESPASSING signs

behind the pool                                       a stream runs through and

collapsed razor wire squares the chemical pond       it's 2018 and backhoes have torn at

my shiver   my urge to wade in          the earth   scraped   the residue stuck

to my insides   I can't rely on                                      memory

or ask my dead

a thousand miles away                          the satellite maps        refresh

to see the diving board sticking out           tomorrow I'll zoom close

the deep end   we count the steps                  pale tongue lapping

100 muddy paces between chlorine and acetone as       from swimming pool to waste pond

the stream                                          children   swam in both and

branches where I hang by the strength of        my body plunging to the bottom

my husband's human face                                my storyteller tail

            On the map                      tells me there isn't always truth

                    it seemed farther

I want to know why                                     he says

why he didn't believe me                      I keep scouring

                                              but the water never recedes

## epiphyte lullaby

in the summered-swamps
there are fuchsia orchids
          budding & they don't give
a damn about you or your blue eyes.

they know the way the sun feels
on their stamens. your focus will wander
          to the murk and stuck-bottomed
boots slurping at the mud.

+

in the crotch of a tupelo tree
          a moss orchid digs its
roots, decides to hold on, to bloom.
          & it still doesn't give a damn

as a mosquito drones over the buds
and body lingering in the water.
          *hold your breath,* the swamp
doesn't need you here.

# Stone Claw Crabbing

*Tavernier Key, FL*

Five-foot waves hid the cages
soaking on the ocean floor,
      braided ropes grew
slime-green in the underwater sunlight.
      Buoys bobbed slightly
while the boat bounced
in the ocean like a rubber duck

in the bathtub, wobbling
to stay afloat. Two sets of hands

worked to hook and pull
the sunken trail markers

off the ocean bottom. The cages,
holding the question of emptiness,
      were hoisted portside.
Among the pig's feet and bait
      ballyhoo, the crabs' broad
bodies lay like treasure, their mouths open,
revealing bubbles. When my father reached

inside, he fought with the crabs

for their arms. He snapped them off
at the shoulders on the bucket's ledge,

then tossed the bodies, back to the broken sea.

## ANNE CORAY

# Mausoleum

*The world dies over and over again but the skeleton always gets up and walks.*
~ Henry Miller

Whatever nature was
it is no longer; already lost
is Australia's short-tailed hopping mouse,
the Carolina parakeet and Hawaii's
moa malo. This is the short list.

Sure to follow is the Chinese river dolphin,
the Philippine eagle, the mountain gorilla,
the giant panda. Bioreserves do nothing
to halt the human population.
They will always be too small.

The question now is whether to let the dead
rest in the shelter of leaf and ground
or to enshrine them. I suspect the latter—
to salve our longing to marvel and touch
we'll dig up bones, scrounge scattered fragments,

and in the great museums, our modern
mausoleums, we'll erect thousands
of lavish temples, rebuilding each vertebra,
femur, mandible, and rib until we have something
that looks like it could walk. Or fly.

Or perhaps redie. It doesn't take long
for reconstruction, and soon enough
a new belief will flourish; we'll know it
as *kampfgeist,* fighting spirit,
that even through this Holocaust survives.

## MARGO TAFT STEVER

# Ballad of the Dolphin

*Ancient Greeks said they should be treated as humans; their sailors would not kill dolphins.*

How I have thought of you
caught in the fishermen's nets—

they would set them to trap
you to catch the tuna

that swam under your schools.
How the fishermen hung

you still alive, upside down—
your cries brought others.

Fishermen grabbed you by
your tails, strung you, and turned

you, head down in water, tied
you to lifting hooks,

and dragged you to the docks. If any
of you were still alive when they slung

you on cement, they stabbed you.
How last survivors churned

the water red, leaping in panic,
waiting to die. In a "good" catch,

it took them three days to kill
all of you. How mothers whose calves

were entangled could not lift them
to the surface. They listened to their helpless

underwater clicks and sighs.
How often I thought of the whale skippers

who would radio the location of hundreds
of you, allowing tuna fishermen

to track down your entire pod. Think
of their nets, deep, foaming, wide,

so that hundreds could fit inside. How they
used underwater sound

to confuse and drive you down—
how many of you drowned.

Fishermen did not want to compete
with you, but killing you was not enough.

How they used the screams
of several to slaughter more.

How one of you hangs from the prow,
still alive, calling, calling.

# JEFFREY GREENE

## Lampreys and the Nuclear Power Plant

The air is so still that the massive plume
above the cooling tower resembles
a genie let out, perfume in the blue sky,
guardian of the sandy shoals of the Loire
and tidy vineyards, Sancere and Pouilly,
quilted pastures and chateau grounds,
grazing Charolais, prized cows that look
like cement. But make no mistake:
this is a heatwave and one wonders
how warm waters warm at the outtake
hurt the fishes and recent comebacks,
beavers known as *castors*. No worries.
Monster catfish snap up sipping pigeons
and ancient carp oblivious to wars and
rubble of bridges cruise the currents.
None can match lampreys, biologists'
wonder, jawless funnel of teeth,
barely vertebrate, not to suck stones
as the Latins would have them but
latch to the bellies of fish, salivate
anticoagulants. What other creature
could keep the cult of taxonomy alive,
the cousin hagfish with a skull and
no spine. By the power plant
fisherman net or trap them, cut
and bleed them, remove their heads,
mix their blood with wine.

MICHAEL GARRIGAN

## Sturgeon Moon

An osprey sweeps thin the sky above us,
        a dead native fallfish splayed across rocks.
We interrupted dinner dragging plastic
        kayaks against river bottom, with
stumbling cursing grunts through shallow water.

This would be worth it if the bass were biting
        like they should be. But they're not.
Neither are the sturgeon since they are gone from these waters.
        Dams, chemical sprays, lawns, macadam, non-natives.
We don't belong, yet here we are
        celebrating the moon and waters
        that are still named by ancestors,
        the ones-here-first, or maybe second.

I like this not knowing
        the distinct lines
between native, wild, invasive.

        I gather in this blur of identity
        and become a star that is only seen
        after a heavy rain in the Badlands on a new moon
        night, clay saturated, steps thick and heavy, the Milky
        Way stretched quietly across the butte.

                    Here I am

        still grunting, feet still in water,
        dragging kayak across rock,
        watching osprey, looking for bass.

# TODD DAVIS

## Until Darkness Comes

*A 100-year-old gray and ductile iron foundry in Somerset, PA, has issued a
closing notice to workers, according to local reports.*

The white blades turn the sky: red-
eyed turbines blinking away the danger
of flying things. Small children float up
over the Alleghenies, parents chasing
the dangling ropes of weather balloons.
It's hard to predict when a storm may blow through.
A boy huddles by a bedroom window, wonders
if his father knows where every deer hides
on the mountain. It's his job to pull the sled
when his father makes a kill. He's been taught
in school the wind that circles the blades carries
electricity to the towns where steel was made.
Three years ago his sister disappeared in the clouds,
heat lightning like veins in the sky. She sends a letter
once a month with a weather report and money
their mother uses for an inhaler. Most of the coal dust
has settled, but fires burn on the drilling platforms
and the prehistoric gas smells like the eggs that spoil
in the hutch when the hens hide them.

The boy never wants to leave this place. Everything
important is buried here: his grandparents; a pocket knife
he stole from his best friend; the eye-teeth of an elk
he found poached at the bottom of a ravine. Yesterday
in the barn a carpenter ant drilled a hole. The boy bent
to the sawed-circle and blew into it, breath forced down
into darkness. He dreams each night of a horse galloping
from a barn, mane on fire like a shooting star. He prays
for a coat sewn from pigeon feathers, for small wings
to fly over the tops of trees where the children land
when their balloons begin to wilt. On summer evenings
barn swallows careen like drones, gorging dragonflies
that skim the swamp. The birds' blue shoulders cant
and angle, breast the color of the foundry's smokestacks
as they crumble beneath wrecking balls and bulldozers,
extinguishing the mill fires the boy's grandfather was sure
would never go out.

# MICHELLE BONCZEK EVORY

## Advection, Nova Scotia

It floated in on the edge of our sight
like the ghosts of lost animals. We watched

it gather on the ocean, drift over white steeples,
red houses tiny as Monopoly pieces

on the peninsula below. We were eating
lunch on the peak of Mount Franey, a peach,

an apple, while it pushed its way up the peak.
On the trail, it closed us in

like puffs of smoke, like a bright moon
vaporizing. A strange bird

pecked at gray grasses. Everything had become
a shade of gray and we walked like shades

through these shades, the dark figures
of trees emerging like soldiers from white

fields, their rifles in their cradled arms shining.
We saw we swore we saw a pink shape

in the distance. An umbrella, a circle
of people looking down at a map. They pointed

at us and we pointed them in the direction
of the cliffs. That is where they needed to go.

A young boy dragged a stick leaving the forest
behind. Willows hovered rootless and we

floated beside each other, our gray faces and
dark eyes looking into what light remained.

Drops drizzled down my chin, down the insides
of my thighs. Our hands met and though they were

too wet to hold, we slipped into each other,
into white woods where we'd heard the calls

of moose, their bellows deep in our bellies,
wings from the grasses their antlers rising.

# NICHOLAS BRADLEY

## Provincial Letter

*...the sky cleared as if the white sediment there had sunk...*
~ Virginia Woolf, *The Waves*


And when at last the rains end, shadows flare
up and water chases water, the rivers

of rivers on Vancouver's sodden Island
inundating already flooded banks

although the glaring light at mid-morning
is frozen. The croaking bird is frozen too,

its branch iced over. Muscled rivers flex
and bulge; every other becomes another.

The far bay, where flattened, sliding current
runs its course, is *mezzo-forte*. Here the high

falls clamor rather rudely as the glum
crow opens his mouth soundlessly before

admitting rank defeat.
What intelligence dapples lank trees

on the northern shore and flickers on thin
crusts of snow above rapids? Is it

only the unembarrassed sun, or is
January's brilliant abstraction

an attestation that rivers, the bird
and its bough, inlet and tide all listen

to rivers and birds, to trees, to tides,
to falls, rock, light? As skies clear, as if white

sediment had sunk to the stream's
rumpled bed, the cold Puntledge and the cold

Tsolum ferry the debris of mountains
and forests to the strait, a belated

owl *who-who*ing. And home now I compose
a missive to my napping son that someday

I may finish. This afternoon it contains
crude instructions for spotting piney

finches as they melt into the canopy,
for knowing how little words say of rivers

and islands. The sublime lies all around,
as familiar as the tousled, trodden ground.

He sleeps; I write; we make no sound.

# BRIAN BAUMGART

## Barren

In so many circles,
there is no word

less desired
than barren:

empty bellies
and sand-fields,

infertile.

What had been
hasn't grown

back.

But we play wizards,
trust in magic

to restore, recreate
luxuriance, the breathing

of microbes like
miniature gods

blessing soil, blessing
seeds: pathway

to renewal.

## D.A. LOCKHART

# Waabiishkiigo Gchigami Stills Herself in the Presence of the Pelee Islander II

She stills herself, body like Erie
Street cement, punctuated by ridges,
ripples of the tension cast by wind
patterns. Know that resting gulls shall
be tossed in the fury that must follow.
Now they bob languid in surface eddies
of a loading ferry, this steadying
of evening performed by new monarch
as she floats dockside. At rest before
the last mainland run of this ending day
from this island, both lake and boat
are indifferent to three passing bikers,
I want them to make note of those
choosing to leave before another week
sets in. Survivors are those that weather
a still lake, a nasty northwestern clipper,
the steady rise of lake waters. We live
our lives as if this stillness that proceeds
departures is the world each of us shares.
Yet, we live in between. Know the Neutral
Sea reflects a white and two-tone blue hull
with gold foil windows that is the boat
of consequence here at the edge of a nation.
Subtle, rippled, a near mirror to the world
above our sea hints nothing of lake bottom
littered with shipwrecks and front over
Michigan that shall unleash a poorer fate
for the gulls that bob leisurely in the space
between closing car deck and concrete dock.

# Mercedes Lawry

## Biodiversity

There is migration, for example.
There are paintings, Audubon's birds,
and others.  Bright photographs
of zebras streaming through tall grass,
dreaming bears.

The neighbor's cat yearns on my porch.
High in the eaves on the side of the house,
the wasp nest grows, a slow bloom.

The fires of Mexico burn for weeks.
Trees keep falling, rain disappears.

My peas are growing well, the red poppies
have exploded.  The basil's sprouted
despite the chilly nights.

The same white moon burns over the ice floes.

What is invisible is equally true.
The extinct are still with us as the imaginary.

MARTHA SALINO

# When I saw the loblolly pine,

its furrowed bark, I knew I was close
to fully understanding when a bird
is gone it's gone, the last one,
*the end, done*, as my daughter
used to say, like the Carolina Parakeet,
menace removed from having a name
in Seminole: *pot pot chee. Kelinky*
in Chickasaw. Pest that got in the way
of tobacco and cotton, adornment
for a lady's hat, an index card's
worth of grief. Their greatest fault:
returning to the place where one
had been shot, otherwise known
as unfortunate flocking behavior.
From the perspective of the moon,
it looks familiar, doesn't it? Returning
and returning to the small-scale
garden plot where your dead brother
lay, scent of dying like a rotting rowboat
beside the Pascagoula Quik-Mart.
There's no fundraiser big enough
to bring them back, no amount
of money to pledge. Because
they loved corn, tore open
apples to reach the seeds,
because their distress calls
could be heard for miles,
there's a little less wonder
along the Perdido River.

## SUSAN COHEN

### Natural History

*It seemed natural to be alive back then.* ~ Jack Gilbert

If there is a place where being alive
seems natural, it should be here
in the bright gravity of a mountain,
its hollows still wet with snow in June.
Sunset rouges the clouds.
Somewhere near, a stream
goes about its enterprise.
Wind sizes up some sugar pines
while a bug takes me for natural,
landing to nurse on my salt.
Once, I sat on a ledge above a valley,
faced by an immensity of peaks.
I was alive but momentary,
relieved at the size of my unimportance.
Back then, I mostly sat in cafès
complaining life was hard
when life was hardly anything.
Those friends are gone.
To be somewhere between sky
and dirt seems enough now that death
feels more and more natural.
The mountain is alive tonight, full
of stream sounds and bats. A dog barks.
The spring snow that dazzled me
melts into the dark.

# Where Will You Go When Things Get Worse?

Surf keeps overwhelming the remains
of a fishing boat beached and abandoned
weeks ago, rubbing it to extinction
wave by wave, plank by plank.
I joke this must be the ship of state—
humor being a vehicle for escape.
If you're an astronaut, you can seek
another planet for atmosphere.
If you're a wordsmith,
you can keep hammering, or else
stop and pour the single malt
to shake you nightly off your axis.
I watch sanderlings, tiny birds
who feed on tides—somehow unscathed
by pounding—and I imagine flight.
But once launched, what Arctic
would I land in that isn't melting?
At my feet, red carcasses of crabs,
a shell being another vehicle
that will take you only so far.
If you're a crab, you can swim
or scuttle, or hunker down
on your unsettled patch of sand,
all ten legs set to resist.

# Gwendolyn Ann Hill

## Memorial for the Future: Climate Chronograph

I. Backyard, Fayetteville, AR

I stopped
taking down growth data
19 days ago.
I couldn't find
my keys. Couldn't remember
where I put
my umbrella. Forgot
to wash my hair.
It wasn't until a wren
flew by with food
for new mouths
that I realized
the problem
wasn't spring
taking too long.

I pull the smallest
from the soil, roots
lifting easily. This pea
one of the first seeds
I planted this year.
52 days ago.
Under ideal circumstances,
peas can reach
almost six *feet*
52 days after breaking through.
It should be flowering
and preparing to fruit.

The tiny seedling, barely
six *inches* tall, is so stiff
I can scarcely bend
the stem. Tinged
with bile, brown spots creep
up crisp leaves.
Fusarium wilt, product
of poor drainage
and flooding.
The fungus invades
the vascular system;
it can no longer
take up water.


II. East Potomac Park, Washington, DC

A grove of cherry trees
will be planted
on a graded field,
close to the sea.
As levels rise, salinity
in the soil will kill
the trees, row by row,
foot by foot,
until they all wither.

I hope to have a daughter
to take there, someday. Dress her
for a picnic in the Capitol,
tie her curls up in bows.
Wet the soles of our shoes
as we toe the line where cherry
blossoms once thrived. Uphill,
we will find few remain.

## VIVIAN FAITH PRESCOTT

# How to Survive a Glacial Meltdown

Acquire animal skills.
          Become a loon, a haunting crier,
swallowing the remains of this world underwater.

Learn to skin. Yourself.
          Pull your feathered hood
over your head, adjust your chinstrap

to your throat.
          Know where the sacred places are,
because there is no

safe place. Your homeland is melting
          at .25 millimeters per year.
 The ocean fills your boots,

there is too much salt in your food,
          and the sandfleas are hopping
on the linoleum.

Lately, you find yourself curling
          up into the dark, nesting near
the water's edge, the place

where your dense bones
          park your truck and watch
the ocean jump the harbor's breakwater again.

What it is that has awakened in you?
          Your tremolo wavers
and the frequent hard rains

now sound like deer hooves—a clack and cry harmonic.
          You know what I mean by that—
you want to run and fly at the same time.

## JACQUELINE KOLOSOV

## Repair

Errand spirits—Mal'ach,
seraphim, cherubim—we have need
of you. The shit-flanked cattle
in the feedlots lift their heads and cry out.
Theirs is a red song. Look down,
come down, find the coyote,
the doe, the opossum gnawing its leg
in a trap. Remember the blue whale,
the gray whale—each day we bar their way.
Ask God to teach us not to fear
the star-gleam in the wolf's eye,
to praise mouse scratch, song
sparrow, and the mule's long ear.
Here, always, the car alarms; here,
always, so much noise. Help us
slice through the red words, red acts,
the sword's edge become poison gas.
Michelangelo never depicted this.
Banish plastic from the gutted soil,
spare earth the shanty towns, teach us
to clean up our mountains of trash.
Are you not spirit, light, the air
we would fall into? Tell us: is it form
that imperils? Some of us have quiet ears.
Speak, please. No one will blame you.

# JANET BOWDAN

## "American Trees Are Moving West and No One Knows Why"

But only some trees head west,
broad-leaf deciduous ones;
more are heading up to Canada,
the needle species,
the evergreens, in fact
an all-out migration of trees
if we could see it,
trees surging towards better weather
preferences set in a best survival
long-term Darwinian way
changing approach as change approaches
a slow dosey-doe switching partners.
Instead of returning to their place in line
the whole line shifts, the forest floor moves;
the rustle we've been hearing in the leaves,
the cardinals' liquid call to re-locate.
We might see it if we mapped out tree census
data kept since 1938, as forestry professors
have, their theory that "different species
are responding to climate change differently,"
some wanting moisture and following it
as nomads follow hunting and snowbirds
the sun, and others, conifers mainly,
want cooler weather,

good skiing year-round, that cold snap
they aren't getting here,
they'd be lifting up their roots like long skirts
if they could, picking their way through the leafmeal
and so our forests are getting less diverse,
which is a problem because forests are more
than just a lot of trees, they are ecological communities
a mix of species and an interaction
among those species and if we can't see the trees for the forest
we won't have a forest, half of it having gone west
and the other half north.

# LANCE LARSEN

## Aphorisms for a Lonely Planet

1.
How hopeful, shoes left by the door, like a pair of pooches hungry for a walk.

2.
Like a rolling billiard ball we touch the world one green millisecond at a time.

3.
In every dialect of bee, *drone* is a compliment.

4.
All ants on earth outweigh all humans—some truths climb your leg for weeks.

5.
The stripes of a drowsing cat clash with nothing.

6.
For us the sky is air. For birds, a bridge between here and there.

7.
We fill the hummingbird feeder not out of charity but to attract some rubied quickness we know we lack.

8.
One oft-neglected lesson of St. Teresa of Avila, the original flying nun: stay rooted. Whenever she lifted off the ground, thus threatening to re-join God prematurely, her sister nuns yanked her back to earth. And to teach herself humility, she once put a saddle on her back, a bridle in her mouth, and muled through her day, on all fours, a beast of burden.

9.
Dirt doesn't mind that we step on it, just as stars do not pine for our promises.

10.
Wonder is the yeast of the imagination.

11.

"A transgression of air, a vibration of souls." I wish you could read this phrase the way I wrote it: in pencil, on the back of a receipt, when we crossed from one green country to another. I mean my first visit to Wales. After wandering Tintern Abbey, I fell asleep in its brokenness. And later petted a blue dog that belonged to gypsies. Did it rain that day? One of those forgiving mornings when I'm sure it did even if it didn't.

12

When I ride the bus: how green, how prudent, how ecologically savvy! When a stranger steps on: poor schmuck, doesn't he have his own car?

13.

Look at that celebrity soar!—like a worm in the beak of a hungry bird.

14.

To climb a new mountain, wear old shoes.

15.

Foolish reader, still trying to use this poem as a mirror?

16.

Mist knows all the shortcuts but is in no hurry to take them.

17.

If you move an animal's bones, its spirit will follow you home.

18.

I fill the teapot not to slake my thirst but to be summoned by singing.

19.

Once when the world turned rainy, a young girl tied her kite to a scarecrow's wrist, then hurried inside. Returning later, a miracle: a man of straw waving at her, while far above, tugging at its leash, a paper stingray guarded the entrance to heaven.

## Compost

I sing the dreck we make a feculent muck
of saving the kingdom come of clipped

grass whirligig leaves and deadheaded
daylilies Parrot Moon kissing Primal Scream

all mixed with the god forbid of kitchen scraps
corn cobs like the chewed legs of pigs

tomatoes sluicy with vegetal roe the mosh-pit
hair of pineapples topped and here a scatter

of artichoke leaves like a dismembered
armadillo fortune cookies minus the fortune

enough cat kibble to punctuate Ezekiel
sumpy cantaloupes ripe as betrayal

not to mention spent tissues sopped in sneezes
and nosebleeds Sunday papers fat

with want ads and exposés here an *au pair*
who tutors trig and scrubs bidets here a hung

jury jiggered by bribes all of it layered
with bales of peat trucked from Alberta bogs

each week I turn it each week I lift my pitchfork
to decay the ripeness almost intestinal

I'm making a bed for Osiris all things reeky
folded together stars falling nightly

from myth into loam in the shaded heat
of this plot a pair of salamanders twining

striped with fire moist as adultery
steam rising with what is buried like plumes

of heat escaping the dead how do I channel
such desire now I kneel and now

I warm my hands in this funk solstice
and dross offal and equinox if only

this sweet god of rot would hold her breath
if only she'd stop panting my name

## ANDREW HEMMERT

### Junkyard at the Florida-Alabama Border

We leave and leave and eventually
we never come back. We leave and we take
our lives with us, we leave our lives behind.

Here the scenery of shacks and pastures
and roadside sweetgums is interrupted,
for a moment, by this collect of rust,

these sagging metal shapes the grass grows through.
I walk between the rows. Junk hunters
press their faces against dust-dulled windows

veined with cracks, fill cloth bags with rear view mirrors.
They rip steering wheels from their stems, stack
hubcaps in cardboard boxes like fine china.

Up the road, the landscape is the same—
only the signs disagree, and the people
who rooted them in cement, anchored them

in this damp, difficult dirt. The same dirt
into which these vehicles will disappear,
years from now. Without fanfare, without

concern for the drivers whose indentations
still cavern the remaining seats. One of the junk hunters
hoists a bumper onto his shoulder,

carries it out to an old red pickup
in the parking lot, and I want to know
how long until that truck comes back to stay.

I want to stay until the junkyard closes,
learn the names of the guard dogs who curl up
comfortable as night under the fenders.

# MICHAEL HETTICH

## The Ghost Trees

And now a certain kind of scientist says
the weather in various parts of the world
is growing exhausted and just wants to lie down
for a nap, or maybe for a longer dose
of oblivion, so its dreams can be
re-spawned, its creatures large and small
replenished to wildness, the air re-folded
into its invisible origami, even
human language shot-through again
with sap.  In the clear-cut woods—
raw ground and stumps—invisible trees
are learning to move from one place to another,
blurring paths and meadows; the people
who live there call them *fathers who turned*
*away without waving goodbye, and learned*
*to dance slowly;* they contrast them with the boulders
and rocks, who truly know how to dance
in slow time, even as the humans and the creatures
in fur and the creatures in feathers leave
their bodies and all the bodies they passed through
to arrive at now through eternities—but still
we pretend they cast shadows across the ground,
and still we pretend they bear fruit.

## Aokigahara

That forest in Japan where men noose themselves,
The mushrooms white with witness,
Where women slipper between trees,
Seduced by whispers they will soon become—

I would enter that forest to scoop one fistful
Of black soil from the needled floor,
To cull mushrooms safe enough for soup,
To recite aloud the names of loved ones

So those trees might know them.
Let their names seep root by root to other forests.
Let ropes remain coiled in backpacks,
And silk scarves sleep among cell phones in totes.

## CATHY BARBER

### Dumpsters

*After Kelli Russell Agodon's "Fragments of a Dissected Word"*

The move
was cleansing—
we filled three dumpsters
with our dross and dreck,
the dust rising with each
toss, a rust-laden rake, a mud-caked
tennie, a cat-scratched chair,
now too downtrodden
even for Goodwill.
Finally, dead
appliances, printers, hazards
all, set aside for recycling,
now, in our exhaustion
and looming deadline, tossed
on the heap to join everyone
else's trash at the dump,
the rump end of the world
where pests—rats, mice, flies—
scavenge for food in that
manna-laden landscape
of stumps of pears,

baby turds in soggy diapers,
purses with broken
straps and bits of mints
and gum at the bottoms. It
isn't true that one man's trash
is another's treasure—it's
just trash, used junk, and there is
so much of it—frayed pet
collars, cracked drum sets,
pus-filled gauze, vases
upset by errant elbows,
polyester shirts with spurts
of ketchup on the breast.
The trappings of all our lives,
one giant melting pot of mess.

## PAULA CISEWSKI

### The Becoming Game

A loon I can see calls to more loons
I can't. I dip my toe in the water.
I do not walk on the water.

I do not walk away from the shore.
Everywhere, something ecstatic
seems to be beginning, just a bright

feeling in the air I'm not sure I am
invited to. Usually I'm in a city. I mean
usually I'm in a house in a city writing

the poems of an inside person who
frequents the insides of schools and museums,
a little pet-like it now seems to me. Where

the forest meets the shore, some mushrooms
have muscled their way up into being
part of the understory overnight.

Maybe it's not crucial you know this
about me but when I was a kid who
couldn't sleep, I played this game called

"becoming." Panther, egret, rhino, shrew:
I shifted my bones around, growing new
ones where necessary, sprouting feathers

or hooves, whiskers or tusks. Are there people
who don't need to know how it feels to be every
living thing? When you're a woman, people will

say things to you like "Lean in!" or "Think more
like a dude!" and it reminds me I never once
as a child in the dark attempted to "become"

a financially secure grown human being.
This luna moth caterpillar inches its way
along the path I'll follow home. It's fat, nearly

translucent, which means it's ready
to crawl up in a tree and chrysalis. Exactly
the kind of small thrill I won't usually

seek. My instinct is to take it off this beach
which I don't. The patient water all around
and somehow the loon I could see is gone. No

loons and no hoot and no wail and no yodel
and no tremolo. They found each other, I'm
going to assume the silence means.

# James Armstrong

## Oligotrophic

Dead. Cold. Clear
as air, pure
as ice: it takes 180 years
for water to leave this basin,
which means—
says the limnologist on the radio—
if you nose were fine enough,
you could draw a cup and taste the musketry
of 1812, the ashes of Toronto.
The lake remembers more than we do:
blood rinsed from a tomahawk,
carbon from the Cloquet fire,
iron ore in the bowels of the *Edmund Fitzgerald,*
the smell of Norwegian pancakes
from a cabin on the shore of Isle Royale in 1927;
the acrid taste of taconite,
the stink of bloated lake trout, stench of burning
pyramids of sturgeon. Potato peels
from Louis Agassiz's Harvard expedition
of 1845. The heel of a moccasin
awash in Two Harbors
in the McKinley administration.

The webbed feet of a fish duck
at the mouth of the Big Two-Hearted
River, right now, paddling.
A beer bottle tossed
from a party barge last night
in Murray Bay. Sawdust
from the last great white pines
of Grand Island
logged in the 1960s
and ferried across, section by section,
on this very lumber tug
tied to the dock
and leaking diesel.

# MEREDITH TREDE

## New York City Pastoral

I've lived these middle years in a place with trees,
time enough for greenery to take root in my dreams,
but my reverie's still lit by the bright white smiles

of billboard queens, by smoke rings puffed high above
Times Square, or the flamingo-pink skin of a spauldeen
ball as it arcs from the pebbly nub of concrete past

the iron rimmed curb to the trash gummed gutter.
Sure I know the easy flower of dogwood, leaf of maple,
but hemlock, fir, or pine are just evergreens, as every

bird's call and color blurs despite my birdbook guide.
Perfect earth-bound bouquets flourish in neighbors' yards;
all I have are strays dropped by wind or creature to bed

in dirt, warm dirt, piled deep for growth, not the grime
that blackens city window sills. I was taught that what
you put in dirt will not come up clean. The hold for me

is spring's hard bounce of rain on ash can lids, summer
asphalt hot to the step, fall's frantic dance of soot-filled
swirls, every snow a thin clean skin to cover stain.

RACHEL MORGAN

## Child-Sized Pastoral

The cornfields rise
like a sloping sea floor.

There's enough sky
to exceed the late morning.

There's farms,
but no farmers.

It's seven turns
over two hours

until the children's
hospital, where you

announce our arrival
*in the city of towers!*

full of potions, and
needles we pretend swords.

After each visit, we exit
the parking garage

into a kingdom
of endangered prairie

whose only protector
is its destroyer. In the dark,

there's nothing to see,
but you look out the window

and tell me you see birds,
hear a song that goes like

# JIM JOHNSON

## Northern White Cedar

Off Prairie Portage near Basswood Lake
a cedar
four feet in diameter
over a thousand feet of
tangled roots (all those dance lessons
lost) and
over a thousand years old (who would want to
live that long). You can bet
not much to say even then when
one Jacques Cartier paddled by
midlife 1600s
and parlayed a nasal
*l'arbor de vie*. Cedar maybe
waved a frond. Yet Cartier knew
life on the rocks like life on the bog, the scraggly
the gnarly thousand year future was not
life at the lake, fronds reaching out
to the sun, tapering into the stand-up life. Yet
rot resistant, all the years by lake or bog. Then
used for railroad ties, telephone poles
shingles, fence posts, canoes too. Carpenters
liked the smell.  Red squirrels ripped
open the cones, scattered seeds. Deer

browsed the lower branches, hence
the browse line. Swainson's thrush lined
their own nests with
the fibrous bark. When winds tipped
an elder over, a branch
seeking the sun
became a new trunk. Just as you
packsacker, too if you
walk the shapeshifting sphagnum
ground pine, bunchberry carpet
through the sacred cedar woods
and pause
late in the month of May
may you see the calypso, hidden
orchid. May you see.

# Ryan Vine

## To Mornings on Minnesota Point

Through waist-high thimbleberry's
white flowers halfway to fruit
Stella dives and Charley follows.

Like dolphins, the dogs surface
and disappear. We're walking this rocky
path to the lake the red pine pad

with their dying—their golden needles
soft as sand—to see the stone line
last night's storm pushed farther up

the beach, to find new bone wood.
Shorn spruce and white pine still
churn in the waves a hundred yards out

flashing bright, spiked branches, turning
like rim-less spokes. Stella stops
to sniff the air. I throw a stick. Both dogs

crash into the rolling water, each happily
retrieving the wrong one.
I just remembered something. I'll add it

to the list of things I didn't get done.

M. BARTLEY SEIGEL

## Land Acknowledgement, Treaty of 1842 Territory

In deep time and song, infinite nations
under cathedral woodland dome, boundless,
long as memory, tall as a story
spun summer from spring, winter from autumn,
sugar bush from trout stream from wolf hymn, moon
to the sun, salt to sweet sea, all fire,
all the branches swaying, leaf and needle,
soul seed dirt to green to gold, queued to choir.
Then snake, the booze hag jig, the winking eye—
mowed down to cord and plow, built mine and rail,
burnt bar and blade. Give an inch, give a mile,
give a swollen river of blood. Gut shot,
       call it by name. Gone to ground and held on
       mother tongue, obscured, but restored to word.

*Maananoons,* "no such thing as a trash tree,"
just ghost washed hands. Patience is a weapon
is a sign is a wheel is medicine,
but poison, too. Relearn the tell. *Wiigwaas,*
*giizhik, biisaandago-zhingwaak*—can't duck
and dodge the unlearned thing, can't eat a tree.
Can't dance atop a land acknowledgement.
A grave stone by any other name is
less than a prayer. Still, we could turn East,
sing to an Earth thick bearded, burl and boll.
Our voices could kindle to gossamer
green, quick between crow's return and chorus
       frog. Closely now. *Zagaakwaa ezhaayang*—
       the forest is dense where we are going.

# Rosemarie Dombrowski

## The Audubon Guide to Relationships, Plate No. 147 (Night Hawk)

This time, it happened in the north,
someplace where people lose their bearings
after the solstice because everything is dark for days
and the thick of the forest resembles
the disemboweled cavity of a deer
or a tanker that was meant to carry fuel
across state lines,
the sound of what some may describe as
the hard grind of an engine
and what others might say is simply
the hardening of the heart,
something that taxes your resting idle
like the rush of a night hawk
chasing bees into extinction,
one yellow and one black,
both tinged with the sweetness of maple leaves.

ALAN ELYSHEVITZ

## A Lamentation on the Destiny of Waterfowl

*The death of one man is a tragedy. The death of millions is a statistic.*
~ Joseph Stalin


Stalin died the year I was born when Canada
geese still bothered to migrate. In psychiatric
hospitals his enemies had awaited demolition
for years. There they ached with a pedestrian
ache like that of an old house settling down.

In college I dabbled in Russian and mathematics.
Statistics, I learned, slip beneath curtains to smooth
out the blankets in mental wards. Stalin knew this.

On the shoulders of every highway, geese peck
at a threadbare world. Automobiles hit them
or miss—somewhere the numbers are available.
But only speed really matters, only the haste
that propels us to the next brutal act of survival.

# PATRICIA CLARK

## Sibelius While an Oak Topples

I turn it up loud,
louder, to mask

the chain saw's
cough and steady

whine, the noise
of the workmen

hollering, the dull
thuds when one

throws down a chunk
of trunk or limb.

What do we do,
living in this

world—my neighbor
who fears the oak

will fall, crush
his boy where he lies

sleeping. I didn't
make the world

of chain-link fence,
bark collar, leash,

bite of the chainsaw,
the woman on the news

who crept out on ice
to rescue her dog,

then fell through,
scrabbling for a way

out. I, too, wanted silence—
look at me using a melodic

impromptu to hide
horror, kick and bite

of the saw, the dog's
jerk to get away

from the jolt
of what they call

"the correction," and yes,
I think she called

for help, woman who
had laughed at work

with kids on the blacktop
playground (they talked

to one boy on the news).
I am not as immune

from pain as I try
to pretend, my chest

felt sore and I touched
Josie's fur, looking in her

eyes, seeing another
creature trying to breathe,

to play with a ball,
or lie in peace on the rug

when the sun streaks in,
promising to last.

The workmen will grind
the stump when they

finish, and the boy sleeps
on. The woman's dog

scrambled off the ice,
safely, and ran home,

that's how her family
knew to go looking. They sail

another chunk down using
a pulley, thud, ground trembles,

goes still. They found
her body there, shards

broken around the hole.
The children said she

played with them every
day at recess. Even now

Josie's learning not
to bark, just one soft

one to sound an alarm,
then she stops.

## SARAH WOLFSON

# The Propagule

*Like most mammals, mangroves are viviparous (bringing forth live young), rather than producing dormant resting seeds like most flowering plants. Mangroves disperse propagules via water with varying degrees of vivipary or embryonic development while the propagule is attached to the parent tree.*
*~ "Reproductive Strategies of Mangroves," Newfound Harbor Marine Institute*

The mangrove spawn,
a sideways (sort-of)
seed, floats and bobs
in the world where
everything's an egg,
(almost) as for the child
who peered over a nest's
edge and—present!—
three blue eggs so real
as to be candy. He didn't
eat. The mangrove pod
bobs and weaves until
it settles rather than
dives sideways on a
habitable spit of sand,
the propagule a kind of
roving ovary, a buoyant
earth-berry in a way,
(if everything's an egg,
everything has one),
an ore that varies
by territory and weather,
an ur-rover, a veritable
apiary (almost), an ova,
a reed, a doe, a ray, and
a—forgive me—a me.

# TONY BARNSTONE

## American Lumber

*When an American looks at a forest, he sees lumber.* ~ Ralph Waldo Emerson

His mind is whirring with teeth and calculations,
    worries that he holds
like his chainsaw blade at arm's length, but the foreman
    lingers for a while
after handing out the week's pay to loggers
    in tan envelopes.

The stump he sits on doesn't know it's dead: its root-
    hairs still finger through
mulched generations of leaves and—like earthworms cut
    in two—blindly feed.

He thinks of the dirt road to the potholed highway,
    the small town nearby,
the Train Track Deli and Bar where he will order
    a poorboy and share
a pitcher with Mel, who shares his need to get things
    straight at the day's end
with bar table pool, cool combinations of bank
    and backspin and skill
until the final click sends the eight ball across
    the green for the kill.

But things have a way of spinning out of control.
    As he's drifting home
on the asphalt strip, some deejay's chatter starts his
    mind spinning again:
"You Should Be Dancing," by The BeeGees, pay GE
    or it gets cut off,
the flopping finger Rick lost at the mill trying
    to keep a board straight.

And it seems even America is behind
    the 8-ball, with bosses
buying bigger homes and drinking at the gated club
    down by the golf green,
while for guys like him the cost's a tumor you can't
    cut off at the root,
the bank owns him from lock to stock, and though he's
    barreling downhill
and the tires eat the road, they can't carry him out
    of his spinning mind
which wheels from this to that all evening till he crawls
    between the covers,

where he won't embrace pillow or wife so much as
    the shadow behind,
where the world trickles off as the nerve-stars spinning
    behind his eyes take
root and, feeding from an underground stream, branch and
    flower into dream.

# BART SUTTER

## Tumbleweed

On dead-calm days, they're just dust bunnies
Of the desert, but let the wind rise,
And they begin to turn, trundle, tumble.
Are they the ghosts of cowpokes
Who hit the dirt and rolled for cover?
A large one resembles a model
Made to illustrate the way blood circulates.
Lift a small one in your hand,
And you're examining the skeleton
Of your own brain.

Tumbleweeds *are* creepy, aren't they?
Dead, they go on moving. Zombie brush,
They seem like animals—porcupines,
Perhaps, without the porky's charm.
You wouldn't want to pet one. One
Or two seem harmless, but
When they gather in a coven
Or a flying squad gets tangled
In barbed wire, then you understand
How they earned their alias:
Witch weed. Easy to imagine how
They might congregate against your house.
Just one spark and . . . conflagration.

Still, though they be creepy dead,
They carry seeds, and a tumbleweed or two
Spinning across a playa will enliven
A long, monotonous journey:
"Oh, look! Tumbleweed."
Now and then, in wild winds,
A big witch weed will leap from the ditch
And go sailing way off toward the hills.
You'll startle, as if you'd suddenly glimpsed
The prickly ghost of one of those wizened folk who saved you:
That old fella with the birthmark wrapped around his neck,
Who said, "If everything seems dark,
You might be staring into a hole."
Or that bent woman with white hair and square black shoes,
Who said, when you were small and sad, "You look
Like you could use a cookie," and offered one,
And you accepted, as if it were the Eucharist.
And it was. Those moments were seeds
That flowered and fed you so, later,
Instead of staying stuck in your ditch of misery and gloom,
You got up and bumbled along with your life.

# C. MIKAL ONESS

## Inclination

Fruit Day on the biodynamic calendar
And I'm trying to keep my balance digging
on the hillside beneath the apple tree.
We're putting in blueberries. I tip a little.
A clay skull of sod unhinges from the hole,
Breaks free and pulls at my wavering weight.
Bigfoot can uproot and flip a whole denuded trunk
And plunge it into the soil, roots webbing the air
Like the old housetop antennas
That brought us the first walk on the moon.
Finally, we don't know how easy it might be
To change worlds and be as surprised as
A Bigfoot drinking from the stream, like she does,
But by a road that wasn't there before
With a car stopped and an astonished driver
Staring. I'd take off into the woods as well
If I could outrun a deer, live on berries
And bark, and craft a xylophone
With a few branches knitted to a tree.
We know everything but what we can't see,
And what the Smithsonian hides from us.
I think of the photo of the two 19th century
Hunters holding a sasquatch head by the scalp,
Long gun shouldered, machete in hand. But where
Are the bodies? Where is the scat? Science demands
A pickled carcass. The facts can be as elemental
As the beings I serve by packing roots with a shovel
Of compost from this pile and a shovel of peat
From the Fairy Isle, dandelion and nettle packed
In a stag bladder, the manure of a lactating cow

Planted in a cow horn then stirred like a witch's brew.
The gnomes, the sylphs, the undines all come
From somewhere if we usher them in. I pick up
A lump of clay by the hair and toss it to the bin.
In fact, I think those uprooted trees impaled
Into the marsh might be a way in and a way out.
Look at us from any distance. Wouldn't you bury
Your dead elsewhere, take a shit elsewhere, raise
Your children behind the calculus of space if you could
outrun a deer, break its leg from behind and load up
on a few berries? How easy might changing worlds be?

# QUINN RENNERFELDT

## Rosemary

What we'll leave: one snaggle-toothed comb in the underbrush. Lone boot, half-chewed through, acting as cap to a fire hydrant. Endless bobbing bottles dotting the sweltering seas. Perhaps this is when poetry dies. Perhaps I'm the grandmother generation. It is not hard to imagine my daughter's daughter, half covered in dust, her womb a cockelshell of rot and want, her eye a flat expanse of thirsty, white sand. No one left to scatter infertile flowers on her face.

Lingering on it is like running one's hands under a scalding tap. So, let's remember this taste of clean, cold water sipped from a damp wineglass on the patio of a middling Italian restaurant. The smell of laundry wafting out of basement windows on the walk home. And the planes, blinking blessings on the black blanket of the sky. Their small, red lights still a stop-in-your-tracks spectacle for the fat-fisted children between us. The tingle of electricity down every block, how this city's illuminated windows become facets of a winking gemstone in the mouth of a wet cave.

We feel lucky discovering the magic of an evening, ignore the warmth wetting our armpits at nine PM on a Saturday in January, and how The End is unspooling only a few steps from where we've paused to lift a branch to our faces and say *yes, this smells just like rosemary.*

SHELBY NEWSOM

## Zizania Texana

*Texas wild rice, a rare and endangered species of aquatic grass, exists in the spring-fed headwaters of the San Marcos River. Because of its endangered status and declining population, Zizania texana is protected by federal regulations.*
~ Harold E. Beaty

Underwater you breathe,
cling to the flower of male bodies,

tangle like wild rice aquatic
rising to break the surface.

Your stem cannot be broken
or submerged in the act of becoming.

Fed by springs, you were once
subaqueous crab grass.

Now you're a celebration capsulated
sterile in laboratory lighting. Still

you cling to headwaters,
undulate awake to polluted thoughts

of being uprooted from riverbed
ponytail pulled by shame.

Environs clouded by loss
of appetite, unable to thrive

when your ribbon leaves cannot do
what they must to bristle and emerge.

# For the Young

I was not like my sister.
She could not spear a worm, slide it
onto a hook.

One July day
in the Rockies—cloudless,
mosquitoes oozing

over lake, dark envelope
of woods
a breath away—

I tightened
the line between me
and the copper glean nicking

the surface
late afternoon. My father
pulled out his bone knife to say

*come with me.* I followed him
into the woods, loosening the hook
from the rainbow's lip

as I tripped in the shade.
I had never seen him filet
a fish up close.

Fish relinquished, the scales' shine
stung me silent. Words softened
in his mouth as he held knife tip

to tail fin, traced without cutting skin.
*Score swift, like bread.*
He lifted the blade and sliced into

flesh. At the opening, we saw
our mistake. Blood came
and went, whispered

red on leaves.
He reached within
the deep cavity, spilled

a purse of small coins—her eggs.
My stomach ballooned.
I pressed lips together while he emptied

the slick body into the stillness.
Later, carrying our catch
he said it wasn't a loss.

The coyotes combing these parts
would thank us
for feeding their young.

# KAREN RIGBY

## Lemons in August

Mineral green Lisbons poised in the desert.
I'm watching bees drunk with sun. A blistered leaf.
Outside Phoenix, west of the municipal airport,
cicadas drone in the mesquite's shade.
All morning the story on Reuters
is bombing. I'm counting
spent blooms on the vine.
What good are the rosemary?
Orange jubilee scaling uniform walls?
The lemons are courting monsoons.
Acidic. Too soon to harvest. Too late to save.
I've nothing to add to the prophets. Lizards pulse
under jasmine. A lone contrail cuts the sky.

## After Blackberry Picking

We never think of rot when savoring
sweet, but they lie together, an embrace
like thorns: we remain live-limbed and yet streaks
of grey have crept in. We gather and look
into our hard plastic pails, emptier
than our toiling had led us to expect
they would be. We are eating as we go,
placing the berries on each other's tongues,
our mouths wine dark from the harvest of this
invasive with fingers-thick canes that crowd
out the smaller-berried natives. Jam holds
no appeal in this season. What in this
world can be made for keeping? To pick now
is enough—sunburned, scratched, juice-streaked, and full.
The sugar of death on our lips is what
makes the berries sweet. Without it, it is
all just showy display: a purple noise
in open fields to mark the seasons by.

## ELIZABETH ONESS

# Of the Farm

*First Shearing*

Chup, chup, chup the matted wool,
flecked with hay and twigs and mud.
The clipper parts the undulant curls,
nicks the hidden skin. The lamb's
pearly ripples like my mother's
shearling coat. I'd press my cheek
against her borrowed softness.

*Genetic Memory*

Who knows?  The impossible might
be possible. In spring I hold the seed
potatoes the way a jeweler holds
rough stones. I calculate the cuts
that will give me the most eyes.
In August, when I turn the earth,
I know when to delve and when
to lift the fork with its pale gold.

*Writing is a waste of time*

So June and July are spent in the garden.
So I weed. I sow seeds. I admire
the ruby and emerald rows.
When the morning sky blackens
and hail fills the yard, the garden
is beaten by round blades of ice,
industry not withstanding.


*Abundance*

The rhubarb chard flares around
its scarlet ribs and beans swell
on their poles. Dragon's tongue
veins its pale green pods
and cucumbers detonate behind
their pricking leaves. Bolted lettuce rises
in tiers like a wedding cake.


*Putting Up*

I slide the knife along the scarlet ridge,
backbone to rumpled green, and brush
the leaves into the sink. Over and over
the rhythm of work: slip the knife, slip the knife,
fill the sink. Pine needles, bird droppings,
bugs and dirt eddy down the drain.
Standing at the double sink, I shift
my weight from left to right then lift
another load of green to the block.

# Sarah Fawn Montgomery

## Offerings

This place makes us leave bits of ourselves behind—the years of our youth,
a finger in the combine, even the farm when the crops won't yield,
abandoned house overtaken by the wildness it was meant to settle,
prairie grass and the trees moving in, holding things upright.

A hardening happens here, work and weather making us tough and brittle
like cicadas, giving us all we can handle until we are just a shell.
When we think we've had enough we squeeze from the husk
and fly somewhere else, always returning to chirp the same song with the others.

Perhaps the Plains have earned it, the years, the house, our brittle bodies.
These are our hard offerings to this hard place. But we survive,
however marked. There are more years. The house still stands.
And up close, the fallen skeletons are delicate, amber and translucent.

ROBIN CHAPMAN

## Prairie Restoration

*for Jack Kussmaul*

Over the years we've watched
the once-plowed fields of our friend's farm
restored to living prairie—little bluestem
grasses streak hills with color, turkey foot
waves above our head, patches of sumac
glow red in the wake of autumn rain,
needle grass waits for the unwary. In fall,
too, we find the gentians, blue and cream,
where once there was brome grass,
or white pine.

Fire has swept out the brome,
scarred the popples and oaks
of the woods beyond, restored
ephemerals to the understory
instead of garlic mustard.

　　　　　　　　　We've walked
the trails, flinging seed, poor substitutes
for bird flocks, wind, and centuries of rain
of seeds from forbs and grasses that made
the tallgrass prairie stretch across
the Midwest plains.
　　　　　　　　In our autumn garden
I give the asters and beebalm another shake,
go back to trying to count the stripes
on the backs of bumblebees—which one
of eighteen kinds is at work by my driveway?

## GRACE BAUER

### Highway 2 Mirage

This is not the first time you have mistaken clouds
for hills here on the plains, where the horizon
stitches a hazy seam between sky and land
and the eye is free to roam, explore the endless
question of distance with nothing
but a line of fence posts to tell you
someone thinks they own this space—
though wind and weather suggest otherwise.
There is something to be said for human persistence,
an attempt to put down roots—like the grasses
that, in certain light, look like the *flat water*
they named this state after, a grand illusion—
like those clouds that, for a moment, convinced you
they were solid enough to climb.

## Not Quite Nirvana

I have duck taped the Buddha's head
to his rusting body and draped him
with a string of plastic pearls pitched,
years ago, from a Mardi Gras float
into my clinging hands. The repairs
do not appear to have marred the serenity
of his repose. He continues to sit—full lotus—
between the Solomon's seal and sage.

In the neighboring bed the plastic flamingo
has weathered another winter, its pink
less gauche than when I first planted it there,
but still perched in kitschy splendor amidst a riot
of day lilies and weeds both the Buddha and I
choose to accept with equanimity—
or, perhaps in my case, sloth—

content as I feel in this moment
to do nothing but stand, statue-still,
observing the tiny agitation of a hummingbird
who flits, fleeting as a thought, into a pot of impatiens
while on the rickety fence that contains all
of us—and nothing—a jay, blue as sky,
squawks his raucous unlikely *om*.

## LESLIE ADRIENNE MILLER

### Path in the Grass

Even though it goes nowhere, I choose it
each afternoon and march toward the fog
that lays its long thigh on the table
of cool steel where otherwise horizon

would unspool its increments of rule.
When the edges emerge, we can love that too,
but the path in the grass is best in mist
that lights the ravage of the margins.

You have to step down from the road
where the tangle comes up to brush
your elbows, and a flush of blues
fans all its cards at your feet, not blooms

but leaves the color of pillow mints
and blades that wrap your ankles
like snapped whips. Tiaras of wild
carrot blacken at the other end

and hush the little snakes that break
their blue links into stilled measures
when we find one flattened in the road.
Otherwise, we'd never bring

the icon of their gorgeous undersides
this far: how blue the tiny bead of brow
and inside their mouths. Like the bay itself,
alive, they drag their yellow chains

of light along too fast for human eyes
to register the quick, and like the bay too
their darker scales pour. This one,
named for the bit of lace a bride

will toss to hopeful boys in a pack,
died with an open jaw and seems
to us now a creature crying out,
but she, like us, was only hunting

a grassy path, the red tongue flicking
out for particles of air that might
tell her how far the water's edge,
how near prey, danger, mate,

or this smear of blue annihilation
that might have married all three.

## Swamp Apocalypse

Though I live in the land of 10,000
lakes, I'm already planning how I'll thrive
once Nestlé's bought us out. The trickle
through my swamp side plot is full
of beaver scat, but where they took
the popple out, oaks dug in
and kept the sun from sucking
dry the scrub. We're not above
eating the rodents here, but we know
to let the beavers have their way.
The real question is: who's
going to have to learn to use the gun?
The old guy down the road says
he'll keep watch and isn't afraid
to shoot, but he's sure to expire
first, and what it means to be lucky
changes by the hour. Most of us
have never seen a bird like that
said to guide sailors home, said
to invite the most gratuitous acts,
but the swamp will lodge whatever lasts
long enough to come. Sooner or later
everything will show up hungry,
and the beavers are going
to host. We approve the long
gouges in the snow where they write

their ancestral names. We go out now
and sit on their mounds in awe, pray
they'll add volume every year,
and hope the lake they're making
is on its way to something vast.
Don't laugh, you with stilted houses
on the beach: We're here to remind you
that catchy refrain is only a fragment
of the plague song kids unwittingly
sing. The rest is shot through with verbs
you're going to want to recognize
when the time comes.

# JUDITH CHALMER

## Autumn

And if there are sorrows?
Not the duckweed in the dense
sulfurous mud, nor the grumbling

party boat motoring to the dock,
not the clothesline cinched,
or the last open flap tucked neatly

into the tent, not the dog bed,
dampish under the table, or the sticky
branch piled next to the fire,

not the gull raising a baffled wing,
loose feather floating over the lake,
not the tilted tarp or the bandaged

stand of birch, not the rinse bucket
or the ragged cloth—none of these
will mind them. When the book

bag yawns, when the chipmunk
dives, when the young loon feeds
when the songbird preens,

and the fog starts to break and
the web starts to sag, when
the acorn drops and the lichen

curls, when the beetle shines and
the rain jacket drips, would that I,
too, could un-know this longing.

## Wild Grapes near Saltville

Sometimes I have to pick the grapes
growing on a train trestle near Saltville
across from the Superfund site,
and I have to eat them too,
as if they are all there is to eat.
And maybe they are all there is to eat
on a Sunday afternoon in summer
so many birds removed from soldiers
who dug salt nearby, for the war, that war,
and even more birds and deer removed
from wooly mammoths that roamed here,
right here where I can pick grapes
and eat them too, grape by grape,
as I watch a turkey fly across the fence
and land there, there where grass grows
where once so many chemicals spilled
that fear fell off our trees like acorns.

The people whose land this was,
before us—before the factory workers,
the farmers, the soldiers with bayonets—
would have picked the grapes and eaten them,
without thinking about toxic chemicals
or how I would one day be here too,
picking grapes as if there is no tomorrow
and thinking there might be no tomorrow.
These people would have eaten the grapes.

# HEATHER SWAN

## Pesticide VII: Victor

The handfuls of dead bees
she finds after the spraying
are not the worst part
for the beekeeper.
It's the bees still struggling
that gets to her. Limping
in a circle like someone
who's been spinning
on a tire swing for too long,
who then stands—dizzy,
nauseous, stunned.
Their wings shudder,
but they cannot fly.
These insects whose bodies
know the rhythm
of the blossoms,
the changing angles
of the sun, whose alchemy
gives us liquid gold,
whose love affairs
with pistils and stamens
give us apricots,
almonds, melons.
To witness is to be
dredged, she thinks.
What war do we think
we're winning?

*This poem is one from a group of poems which borrow their titles
from the names of registered pesticides.*

# In Which I Begin to Bargain

for my plastic bottle—the albatross
for my 4-lane—seeds unbound
for my cotton quilt—the many years of backs, the many years of hands
for my wireless—some silence
for my tortilla chips—the fields of daisies, the fields of queen anne's lace
for my gas cap—the polar bear, the harbor seal, the tern
for my thermostat—the mountaintops of Kentucky and West Virginia
and for my perfect lawn—frogs
for my insecticide—the songbirds' eggs, the butterflies, the bees
for my fossil fuel—the fossils, the strata undisturbed
for my palm oil—the orangutan
for my mascara—the rabbits, the mice
and for my smartphone—Congo
for my blue jeans—the seamstresses, and their eyes, their children, their hands
for my many myths—the crows, the bats, the rattlesnakes, the spiders
for my jet plane—the coral reef, the mollusks of many shapes
and for my mirror—skies

# JEN KARETNICK

## Flight Plan

*~ at Bill Baggs Cape Florida State Park, for Jennifer Hull*


Because we couldn't take our eyes off the children,
shaking droplets off like anhinga in the sun-greased air,

because I had lost my daughter once on a Naples beach
that year and, already hanging cloth over the mirror

of my heart, thought *Yes, I will forever now be that mother*,
because I had been late but my friend had been later

and the waning afternoon was a hunger we were trying to control,
we spoke to each other as if we were driving, our faces in profile.

Peripheral. We saw only the dangers that lay directly ahead
for the smallest-limbed swimmers among us, who were not

really swimmers yet at all, who were awkward in every medium,
coordinated as windchimes in a hurricane. We didn't notice

the silvering fog of the newly installed mist nets, there to catch
neotropical migrating songbirds at the banding station,

barely visible mesh border walls for tanagers and bananaquit
whose wings couldn't beat them through on the way from

Eastern Canada to the Western Caribbean. Capture, it seems,
is for their own good. Typed, sexed, blooded, they are afterward

let go to feast on the skins of fruits and insects, storing sugars
and proteins in their strong treble bellies for the next leg

of their journeys. Since that summer, 27,402 passerine have been
counted and chronicled, named and noted, some as numerous as

the more than 4,000 ovenbirds, others as rare as MacGillivray's mourning
warbler, of which there has been only one. Now children take field trips

with their mothers to learn about the sapsuckers and flycatchers.
They climb the lighthouse steps, closed for repair when our daughters

were young enough to want to, when our legs were strong enough
to go with them. We wouldn't know any of this as we scrubbed

their cheeks with aloe. Selfish herd. Flock of two by two. Pink sun,
veering together. Mary Oliver wrote that "a poem should always

have birds in it." Perhaps what she meant is that here, in this place,
there can also be no grounding without joy in it. This is how I now see

that day: Each child in our arms. Each bird in its net. The horizon, filled
with its own swelling promise, also waiting for some kind of release.

# ED O'CASEY

## Fruit Stand

not that we don't grow enough food—
merely fruit too ugly
to be sold face-to-face, far too hideous for the shelf:

only good enough to grind into jellies and fillings.
can you imagine?
nuzzling a bumpy peach? getting lip

to skin with a Granny Smith that has lost her green and round?
maybe we should stop shelving based on sweetness and crisp. kind
of like sleeping around with girls for their personalities:

*Single Rhetorical Male seeks loving, generous F*
*for meaningless one-nighter. must love dogs.*
we should select
for melonous curves:
*Hispanic Working Male seeks brackish*
*white cabbages for short-term stir fry.*
we should select for
biochemistry:
*Married Older Dumpster seeks veggies*
*with low self-esteem. do the boys in the field reject you?*

*I won't. no clingers!*
when Eve handed him the apple, Adam
should have been all like,
*get that spotty, lopsided shit out*
*of my grill!!*
instead, he evolved into a hairless ape
obsessed with shelf-life and symmetry.
*MWF*
*seeks artichoke with good heart. must love abundance,*
*take pleasure in immigration law, and meet shelving standards.*

KATHLEEN RADIGAN

## Monarch

In the garden I cup a hand
before you, strain my wrist,
willing you to perch.

A nearby woman grips her cane.
"Young lady. If you touch them,
they die."

Born again from a gauze
coffin, you're blackwinged,
fragile on a wax leaf.

In the heat
of a weeklong life
you batter between

fluorescents and dahlias,
legs thinner than wires,
and float over tendriled

chrysanthemum heads.
Tease everything—hands,
canes, stem, with a feathery

suggestion. I want
to chew you.
Taste the metallic
powder of each wing.
If only to become
so beautiful

that being
touched just once
would kill me.

## GINNIE GAVRIN

### Apple Pie Calculated in New Climate Time

*Every March 14, Einstein's birthday, number lovers raise a piece of pie
in celebration of pi, one of math's most famous constants.*

Earth's garden is shrinking
as memory becomes

a useless arc
no longer a reliable

constant. The way a new
chaos

is changing the ratio
of our emotional circumference

Like Eve we have tasted
our first bite—banished

to a future we made
and cannot see

Our backyard tree fruitless
This year's Fall an irrational

promise of fruit and flower
the way the seasons misalign

Drought and frost out of sync
Blossoms dropping

before bee wings
can be soaked in pollen

The deer wander
in the dark

nibbling at phantoms
We lift an empty fork

# MARJORIE SAISER

## Crane Migration, Platte River

I am in danger of forgetting the cranes,
their black wavering lines in the sky,
how they came as if from the past,
how they came of one mind,
wheeling, swirling over the river.
I am in danger of losing
the purling sound they make,
and the motion of their long wings.
We had stopped the car on the river road
and got out, you and I,
the wind intermittent in our faces
as if it too came from a distant place
and wavered and began again, gusting.
Line after line of cranes
came out of the horizon,
sliding overhead.
The voices of cranes
harsh and exciting.
Something old in me answered.
What did it say? Maybe it said *Kneel.*
I almost forgot the ancient sound,
back in time, back, and back.
The road, the two of us at the guardrail,
low scraggle of weeds flattening and rising
in wind. This is what I must retain:
my knees hit the damp sand of the roadside.
This is what I remember:
you knelt too. We were wordless together
before the birds as they landed on the sandbars
and night came on.

# I've Come Here from the Birds

The crows called me into being,
when I was a three-year-old
sitting on a doorstep.
When the crows made their sound,
a racket in the pines at the edge of the yard,
I paused, my mouth open.
In one hand I held a dish of soft butter
to dip the radish in,
in the other hand the radish, forgotten,
uneaten. Later there were birds with
sweeter songs. Cardinals with melodies,
or snow geese at night calling above the city.
But I began with the caw of crows.
One instant everything was blurred together,
then the scrim lifted, and I became
observer, listener, awake to the world.

# Jessica Turcat

## Instinct

A house wren rests
on the white sleeve of a
sycamore not unlike this house-
wife amid her morning ritual.
Except this place is no
longer my home and here

I am no wife. In the passing
dawns, through the drifting
brume, we regard each other
as if across a kitchen table.
She's perched atop
the floral painted nest box

I nailed to the fence-post.
Last summer, following
the second breeding, she left
that hole; this spring she staked
claim to the front porch
railing. After a rainstorm

subsided I poured a glass
of Bordeaux, watched
as she pecked a tree
swallow to near death a few
feet from my wicker chair.
The defeated bird flapped

forward, one wing pitched
slightly higher than the other,
        paused a moment before
                she caught her harmony.
Cerulean feathers flitted
        in her wake: across the yard


        to the shelter of trees,
then beyond the tree line,
        woodland, deep enough
                to swallow any shadow.
I knew she was the same
        wren, returned.


        Some say leaving is
a lifelong process.
        No point asking
                why a woman stays.
Head tilted, she studies me
        as if to confirm:


*We are Midwestern by choice.*
*We have black walnuts*
        *in our blood. We have moss-*
                *laced rocks beneath our soles.*
For one moment we align
        as equals, every creature:


        rooted, winged, broken,
unconscious, clawing.
        Perhaps it has always been
                this way, except we worry
about the daily trifles
        of putting on and taking

off and stitching holes
we accumulate in the process.
The wren soon shifts
her attention back to
the stalks of peppermint
invading the front beds,

appreciating how victory
dies in the face of hunger.
I've lived long enough
to recognize when
we must question
what we see:

when everything we thought
had been questioned by those
who built the binary systems
dissipates like last night's fog.
Then one morning seven
speckled orbs rest in her roost.

In Scripture, seven—
the symbol of completeness,
perfection. Seven
sacred feasts of Israel.
She's added spider egg sacs,
meshed cottony cocoons

mid tangled coarse twigs with
grass, feathers, pine needles.
She leaves only to feed, drops
curls of cabbage moth
caterpillars to six gulfs until
they want more than she can

suffer. I move to her
corner of the porch;
she dives at my head, circles
a wide parameter, dives again.
I devour her shrill melody.
Admire the grit.

Her familiar hope
to hitch this intruder's
attention with sharp wind-
borne trills. When she fails
to sate their desire, one
by one they forsake her.

How insignificant my possessions
compared with what she teaches:
How to starve. How to lure
death away with archaic song.
How to take flight, without permission.
I do not think she will return.

Alone, I watch a myriad of
spiderlings swarm her
abandoned home, consume
the final—faultless—bedded shell.

## TRESHA FAYE HAEFNER

### Elegy for Wasps

Listen,
there was a wasps' nest in the rafters, just outside the door
to apartment 18 next to the freeway.
In the early mornings, I would stand on the walkway,
attending to the buzz of them building their nest.

It was cool in summer. Mist rose up and fell on the breast
of the hills where the mountain lions tried to rebuild their habitat,
where the wood voles were starting to mate again,
where the jasmine were opening
their white hands in applause for the sky.

My boyfriend and I had just begun our life together in a city
that wanted to chew everything up for itself and blow it apart
like bubble gum.

I was in my twenties, carrying cups of coffee onto our walkway,
drinking in front of the neighbors in just my bathrobe.

But the wasps never complained.
They never forgot something once you told it to them.
They carried your secrets up into the hexagonal structures
of their perfect living geometric dome.

Little Jews building apartments in Florida,
Russian immigrants buying property together in New York.
They were building a structure for their children.
The pupae. The white mucus of first beginnings.

All spring I stood on the walkway in my bare feet, drinking
the sunlight, watching the wasps with their beautiful
smallness shift upwards on the wind, strengthening a home
made out of wood and saliva, their glistening, honeyed abdomens,
like soft yellow and black bullets protruding as they gave up
everything they had to their young.

Then, one afternoon,
our neighbor called the exterminator.

I came home and found the wasps, dead on the walkway,
their grey structure, half-smashed on one side,
but the rest, intricately preserved like a Jew's paper-cutting,
kept and coded from the Medieval ages,
a nest full of larvae frozen in time.

Now we live in a new apartment, smaller,
but more expensive. I sit at my writing desk
watching gum wrappers float along the corridors
between us and the neighbors,
Russian immigrants who came here
alone.

Nothing else has changed for us.
The faces of jasmine open whitely each evening.
The voles give birth. The mountain lions search
for their mates in the hills.

And we're happy, I think.

But the wasps are dead.
Their nest was never finished.
I have its remains on my desk,
next to the pencils and countless sheets
of expensive handmade paper.

These insects, their frozen energy,
their unfinished home, like a tiny,
mathematically perfect apartment
and the mummified body of one wasp
who didn't get out.

Its spindly black legs still kick, like a construction worker
swinging a hammer, or a fireman going back in
to save what is left in the smoke, a mother listening
to the sound of someone calling or singing to her.

The song of all unfinished futures,
the children, the white, delicate larvae calling
to the one who will come back,
to the heart of her giant, papery dream.

KAREN SKOLFIELD

## Keystone Species

The jungle sounds as expected, only more so: greensong, jaw and whoop, thoracic. "If they're looking for mates, how long could that possibly take?" Dennis asks. The guidebook describes food but little else about the countries visited. Eating eyeballs gives bragging rights, but only if everyone else looks a little green. My son stops constantly on the trails, sure the army ants are jawing off parts of him. An international flight creates a larger carbon footprint than 350 homes for a year, my husband reminds me as the "fasten seatbelt" sign blinks on. A man stands in a pile of coconuts and hacks off the tops with a machete; tourists hand him five ringgits, the equivalent of a dollar. Did he have all his fingers? Dennis asks, and I admit I'd had eyes only for my coconut. On the way to Taman Negara, the acres of jungle clearcut and poisoned to plant cash crops. The U.S. has done worse, I remind the kids, and they respond "But the tigers." We call Malaysian animals by animals we know: near-rabbit, souped-up pig, super robin. A half-tame tapir comes to the restaurant every night at 8. There's a bowl of watermelon rinds for the tourists who want tapir selfies. The last known Sumatran rhinos wear GPS chips, as do the last Gila monsters in the Sonoran desert, though the chance of them finding each other is slim. "Keystone species:" never human. My husband's added too many hot peppers to his noodles, but he's determined to clean the plate. The sign at the breakfast buffet is written only in English, not Malay. *Food is life. Take only what you can eat.*

## Sub-adult

Bear-wise, this bear's not much.
Sub-adult, squat trash can, fur dulled
by estivation, hungry as hell.
She's come for the bird feeder
hanging in the oak, four feet
above her full-bear reach.

Can bears jump? We debate.
The feeder's spinning,
fitful spit of sunflower seeds,
a reluctant slot machine.

*If she moved the grill over?*
My daughter's rooting for the bear.
I tell her we don't want bears
on the grill, even small bears stretched
like circus bears, pawing at the air
like she's been taught to wave.

Spring we think of as abundant
but not for bears: no seeds, no berries,
carcasses reshuffled to palaces of bone,
only the ungulates bearing
the bellyaches of rich spring grass.

Over the protest of kids we consider
banging pots, letting loose the dogs.
A fed bear is a dead bear, I tell the kids,
even this bear, all ribby and matted,
its high-gloss gone.

*But what if we . . . oh never mind*
my son begins and ends. The kids
are old enough they know no fight
will make me feed this bear. My daughter
does not say she wants it as a pet,
when her younger self would have begged.

This bear's hungry and we want
to do right by it, we've hung
the bird feeder out of reach,
we're out of ideas, silent with each other,
we've gathered at the window to watch.

## SEAN HILL

# One Saturday Morning

It was spring in Carmel. There were birds. It always
feels like spring in Carmel. It still felt like deep winter
back home in Fairbanks. There were Bushtits and Band-tailed
Pigeons, Acorn Woodpeckers, Western Scrub-Jays
and a Brown Creeper, Black Phoebes, Spotted and California
Towhees, a Townsend's Warbler, and others; a gull floated
high overhead. I stood on the patio in the least layers
I'd worn in months. I held you, legs wrapped by my right arm,
between my wrist and elbow your seat. You'd only recently begun
pointing out the living room window at trucks and cars moving along
the hardpack snow on the road back home. There were birds—
a whole new community for you—, and the American Crow
on the wire was the largest, and so I thought the easiest
for your young eyes to perceive, so I pointed up at it, and you
pointed with me with what was surely my hand when
I was your age, but your eyes didn't follow our fingers.
They looked to me and out and inward like when we
listened to music in the kitchen back home in Fairbanks
with our waving hands in the air, but on the patio there
was no music save birdsong. I pulled my hand back
and jabbed it at the crow, and we're doing an old disco move.
I leaned back with you in my arm and watched your eyes
roll down in your head to stay level to the horizon.
After a couple of tries the crow cawed and ruffled its feathers
at us, and you discovered it. O, your emphatic finger showing me
that there was a crow on the wire—acknowledging that bird
and then others. You revealed not what I knew—that there
were birds one Saturday morning in Carmel—but made me feel
again how the world opens before a curious body—our bodies.

# Sugaring Redux

*for Devin Corbin and Joan Menefee*

Last drop,
cold small globe,
your leave-taking
of the tree slowed
on the metal spout
that funnels a runnel
of sap into the bucket.
On the spile's lip you
hang at the end
of the day like baby
drool—gravid, sweet,
glacial potentiality
desiring gravity, eager
to run with this coming
of spring. I find you
in the first rays
stopped in your path,
you the last at day's end;
you waited all night
in an orrery of some
system beyond our
knowing in this grove,
points plotted, orbits
like swallows
in meadows
and the fire
beneath the kettle
kept aglow always
the daystar's proxy
till its return
and you fall away
with your brethren
sap planets plopping
into the pail
first drop today.

## SARAH CAREY

## A Pileated Woodpecker Shares Where to Find God

I live for what the dead give.
Hidden by leaf screens and branches,

I pillage rotting wood. My tribe fought
long for salvation, after the forests' razing

dug into ragged stumps, felled trunks,
a miracle of wholeness from fragments,

a feast of insects who thrive on decay.
What's left when I leave is for others to say.

Should you see my black wings
and red head knocking wood for nourishment,

you might ask if I believe God is dead,
as Altizer said, believing God lived and died

in Christ, that the church lied
about becoming the body—but what Altizer said

was not what most thought he meant,
which was in death, life—a spirit

indwelling to drill the dying down,
incarnate carnage, God's passion.

If you ask me, I'm proof he was right.
If you listen to my rat-a-tat melody

echoing my drumming beak, you may hear
an answered prayer of oneness, in desire's

shrill tattoo, and the thrumming
of your own wild heart.

# Fleda Brown

## Felled Tree

Dear swollen-trunk maple, deemed
diseased by the saw-happy tree guy,
you who have stood silently, supposedly
slipping your ailment through your roots
to the neighboring trees, now fallen
full blast down, geometrically down,
right angle, then parallel at last, your flat-
sawn stump blotched with incriminating
evidence—you came and leafed
and are gone, and I who have grown old
in your lifetime, who intuited you rather
than knew you, felt you in my bones,
now feel the slightly thinner woods,
the hint of frailty. Scott the tree guy
has carried your eighteen-inch logs in his
red wheelbarrow and stacked them
for winter: a little Williams, a little Frost.
    Oh tree, everywhere I look
I have to pledge reclamation, fill
the forest floor with ferns, mushrooms,
pine needles, and in the side corner
place the outhouse, practically unused
anymore, still in good shape, emitting
its rich human-waste smell, its wood
smell, its few spiders climbing
their trellises with their sticky feet.

Oh tree, so much has been discovered
to fill in the space where you were:
seven new species of Philippine
forest mice, a new genus of blind
Bulgarian beetle, four new species
of jewel beetles, six of New World
micromoths. I have filled my note cards,
I have left the vertical space open
for the Ur-tree, the canonical vision
that will take your place, even the stigmata,
your bulged and arthritic joints, the
whither of your leaving, the grand word
*whither* standing where you were.

# ALESSANDRA SIMMONS

## What Was Created Still Exists

On the first day there was light and the light was good and the light rotted the folds in the cotton curtains and the deck furniture faded from orange to yellow and then to dust

On the second day there was water and heaven and they were both good and waves crashed upon the heavenly shores and like a child playing with wooden blocks the waves rearranged coastlines

On the third day there was dry land and the land was good but lonely so fruit sprouted and then bowed down in the form of a seed and the seed was swallowed by the land and because light and waves crashed upon the seed it appeared again as fruit and the fruit fell from the tree and rotted on the land and the fruit became soil

On the fourth day the moon pulled on the seas and the moon was good and the seas grew hungry for dry land and the houses that were built cliffside were reinforced with concrete pillars and waves gnawed concrete until rebar showed and the houses were threadbare

On the fifth day there were birds, fish and phytoplankton and the birds ate the fish and the fish ate the phytoplankton and phytoplankton were chained to the sunlight swilling around the seas' surfaces and when the birds died their bodies fell into the sea and the scavenger octopus devoured them and when the fish died their scales drifted down shifting like snow and the squid and jellyfish combed the flakes into their dark mouths and it was good

On the sixth day there were animals and the animals were good and rabbits burrowed into soil and deer tugged on prairie grass with flat teeth and racoons hunted for berries and bison took naps on warm railroad tracks so men riding trains with their shotguns resting on the open windows shot them and piled their carcasses north of the tracks and soil centipedes and dung beetles climbed up the mountain of rot and the vultures and crows circled the decay and pulled at the flesh and the sun whittled their bones into gravestones and toothpicks and the rains poured down on the seeping hill and carried the bones and tufts of fur like tiny ships navigating spring rivers

On the seventh day there was rest and men hung in hammocks and women washed dishes with their hands submerged in warm sink water and scrubbed each pan with steel wool for longer than necessary and children hunted grasshoppers in the tall grass and grasshoppers chirped and the children fell eye-to-eye with the insects to inspect where the sound had come from

On the eighth day there was polypropylene and it was heated and poured and it cooled in the shape of chairs and TicTac boxes and pill bottles and cell phone cases and it was spun into rope and windbreakers and sheets of it were cut into the shape of diapers and disposable lab coats and sometimes the chairs broke, or the windbreakers went out of style or the rope wasn't needed and cellphone cases wore through and the pill bottles and TicTac boxes emptied and sometimes these things were carried by the wind like seeds and crushed at rush hour in the streets or sometimes they were piled in shipping containers or landfills and were made brittle and discolored by the sun and sometimes the waves ground them into fragments that filtered through soft bodied sand crabs and they became lodged in the throat of a night heron and sometime they rode the seas like the shadows of phytoplankton and sometimes their particles tried to break into their component parts but could not and never was there anything to digest them

# KIMBERLY BLAESER

## Eloquence of Earth

Nominal signs, these words we use—*future, ecology, seven generations*—
have yellowed into clichés, editorials that line the cages
of captured birds, burn in unransomed stone fireplaces
of America's aspiring, royal mining families.
These green futures cast as fairy story,
sealed beneath the calloused ideals of legislators—
sleek smiling handshakes who seal bargains like Jabez Stone;
Our *I-do-solemnly-swear* paper-promise leaders
enticed by industry frenzy, slight of lips,
the short-sighted tally (seven hundred jobs)
coveted like Stone's seven years of prosperity.
Though publicly professed (*against all enemies, foreign and domestic*),
and leather-oath sworn (*will bear true faith and allegiance*),
still *quid pro quos* reign, sell the soul of this land—
our waters our *manoomin* our children, *abiinoojiihnyag.*
Each season gavels strike new bargains with our oldest enemies
*maji-manidoog,* handsome fast-talking strangers disguised as prosperity.

Daily we watch patient warnings swim the Wolf River,
wash up on the shores of our great lakes,
migrate to absent wetlands, trumpet old calls.
How do we translate the flashing fins of poisoned fish?
What other alphabet do you know to spell *contaminated waters*?
Like banned books words still burn on my tongue—*reciprocity,*
sacred, preservation, earth, tradition, knowledge, protect.
Even the vellum of *justice* disdained, crumbled in quick greedy fists.
Meanwhile we gather here, descendants of *ajijaak* and *maang*
lift our ancient clan voices in longing, for a chant of restoration
in a Faustian world.

If I say *Gichigami—Lake Superior—a turquoise plain, stretches*
*infinite, gete-gaming.* If I say *Wiikonigoyaang, she invites us to her feast,*
how many will remember the eloquence of earth itself?
At dawn when *jiibay* mist backstrokes across the copper of northern prairies
eerie white hovering, damp and alive,
will you stretch out your hands in hope
cup the sacred like cedar smoke,
draw it toward you—a gesture
fervent and older than language?
Now I say *wiigwaasikaa,* everywhere we look
there are many white birch,
bark marked with sign, scrolls a history.
I say *ritual, continuum, cycle of belonging,*
I say *daga,* please; *ninandotaan,*
you must listen for it—*aki.*
Yes, our very earth speaks.
Who among us will translate?

# CAMILLE T. DUNGY

## Trophic Cascade

After the reintroduction of gray wolves
to Yellowstone and, as anticipated, their culling
of deer, trees grew beyond the deer stunt
of the midcentury. In their up reach
songbirds nested, who scattered
seed for underbrush, and in that cover
warrened snowshoe hare. Weasel and water shrew
returned, also vole, and so came soon hawk
and falcon, bald eagle, kestrel, and with them
hawk shadow, falcon shadow. Eagle shade
and kestrel shade haunted newly berried
runnels where deer no longer rummaged, cautious
as they were, now, of being surprised by wolves.
Berries brought bear, while undergrowth and willows,
growing now right down to the river, brought beavers,
who dam. Muskrats came to the dams, and tadpoles.
Came, too, the night song of the fathers
of tadpoles. With water striders, the dark
gray American dipper bobbed in fresh pools
of the river, and fish stayed, and the bear, who
fished, also culled deer fawns and to their kill scraps
came vulture and coyote, long gone in the region
until now, and their scat scattered seed, and more
trees, brush, and berries grew up along the river
that had run straight and so flooded but thus dammed,
compelled to meander, is less prone to overrun. Don't
you tell me this is not the same as my story. All this
life born from one hungry animal, this whole,
new landscape, the course of the river changed,
I know this. I reintroduced myself to myself, this time
a mother. After which, nothing was ever the same.

## Spotted Wing Drosophila

Carried here on a hurricane
and kept alive by warmer winters,
these fruit flies just want to multiply,
find a home for their young.

When the slant of sun says spring,
they search for the softest skin
of cherries or nectarines to sting
and place their eggs inside.

We blame them for ruining crops,
for decimating the raspberries—
no more dew-slick jewels
hidden among thorns, no more

pies, tarts, or jams—the fruit
gone soft with rot as larvae
feed and grow inside, unaware
of the damage their living brings.

Yet like us, they have simply
staked their claim in nature,
taken over what must seem to them
nothing but ripe sites for breeding.

And don't we do the same
when we clear a tract of land
of towering pines and sumac,
of fox dens and mouse nests

and the mole's intricate tunnels,
just to build a house with a view
and move ourselves closer
to the mountains we say we love?

## KIMBERLY ANN PRIEST

### at the butterfly habitat

*Complacency and false-positive assumptions about the resiliency of once-common species can have tragic consequences when timely action is not undertaken to safeguard their populations.*
~ Center for Biological Diversity

Cruz points to a stalk of milkweed and explains that this is monarch food.
We are surrounded by a former cornfield now turned into small farm plots
for refugees and food banks, and this butterfly habitat.

He cuts me a stalk and feeds it through the mouth of a used water bottle
we find in the field and fill with well water; then holds up
a monarch caterpillar in a cup. *We have to manage them now* he says,

waving a hand out at the field that requires constant tending to keep weeds
from overtaking the newly reinstated native species. The caterpillar
munches voraciously on small leaves protruding from a small stick in the cup.

Cruz gives me the milkweed and the cup and begins searching a tomato plant
to find the large praying mantis he located earlier as he explains that they eat
both lady bugs—a helpful species—and other bugs destructive to his struggling

native plants. The mantis is undiscriminating, he says, but
he lets it be and *takes one for the team.* (He means the ladybugs.) We don't find
the mantis, so my tour culminates in an invitation to weed the land anytime

as Cruz points to and names various invasive plants that threaten the habitat
so I will know what to pull up and what not to. I use my phone's camera to
photograph the weeds—data for when I return. But, for now,

I will take the caterpillar home, feed him milkweed, watch him cocoon
and set him free full-winged. *He will do a little dance,* Cruz says, *to test the air
before flying.* The whole process meticulous—man, insect, plant.

I look out at the work he has done, at what appears to be a tatty field—not
the raw resources of butterfly survival, slightly pleased that I can do something
for this lone would-be-monarch—already sick, already dying in my cup.

## protections

Against the whir of my treadmill,
       a shot rings out,

and a wolf is gunned down—O-Six
       they named her.

*Numinous* alpha female
       of Yellowstone National Park

because she survived
       solo.

Even the commentator says
       this was unusual

and dangerous; yet she was beloved
       for acuity

and beauty, face like an owl mask against
       snow white.

I listen as the hunter celebrates
       his kill, the documentary

rolling. My treadmill
       rolling.

They had lifted the ban on hunting
       wolves that year—

*endangered* status long enough
       for a female

to become her own pack, survive, surpass
       the males of her kind.

## A Sighting

The gray owl had seen us and had fled
but not far. We followed noiselessly,
driving him from pine to pine:
*I will not let thee go except thou bless me.*

He flew as though it gave him no pleasure,
forcing himself from the bough,
falling until his wings caught him:
they had to stroke hard, like heavy oars.

He must have just eaten
something that had, itself, just eaten.
Finally he crossed the swamp and vanished
as into a new day, hours before us,

and we stood near the chest-high reeds,
our feet sinking, and felt
we'd been dropped suddenly from midair
back into our lives.

# JOY HARJO

## Eagle Poem

To pray you open your whole self
To sky, to earth, to sun, to moon
To one whole voice that is you.
And know there is more
That you can't see, can't hear;
Can't know except in moments
Steadily growing, and in languages
That aren't always sound but other
Circles of motion.
Like eagle that Sunday morning
Over Salt River. Circled in blue sky
In wind, swept our hearts clean
With sacred wings.
We see you, see ourselves and know
That we must take the utmost care
And kindness in all things.
Breathe in, knowing we are made of
All this, and breathe, knowing
We are truly blessed because we
Were born, and die soon within a
True circle of motion,
Like eagle rounding out the morning
Inside us.
We pray that it will be done
In beauty.
In beauty.

# CONTRIBUTORS

**Michelle Acker** is a Florida-based poet and a recent graduate of the Creative Writing MFA program at Hollins University in Roanoke, Virginia. Her work has appeared or is forthcoming in journals including the *Florida Review, Gesture, 2River View, Permafrost, Saw Palm, Poetry is Dead, Spilled Milk,* and elsewhere.

**Kelli Russell Agodon** is the cofounder of Two Sylvias Press where she works as an editor and book cover designer. Her most recent book, *Hourglass Museum,* was a finalist for the Washington State Book Awards and shortlisted for the Julie Suk Poetry Prize. Her second book, *Letters from the Emily Dickinson Room,* won Foreword Indies Book of the Year Prize for poetry. She coauthored *The Daily Poet: Day-By-Day Prompts for Your Writing Practice* with poet Martha Silano and is the co-director of Poets on the Coast. Her next collection of poems, *Dialogues with Rising Tides,* is forthcoming from Copper Canyon Press. www.agodon.com

**James Armstrong** is the author of *Monument in a Summer Hat* (New Issues Press), *Blue Lash* (Milkweed Editions), and *Nature, Culture and Two Friends Talking* (North Star Press). He teaches English at Winona State University in Winona, Minnesota.

**Stacey Balkun** is the author of three poetry chapbooks and coeditor of *Fiolet & Wing: An Anthology of Domestic Fabulist Poetry.* Winner of the 2019 *New South* Writing Contest as well as *Terrain*'s 10th Annual Contest, her work has appeared in Best New Poets 2018, *Crab Orchard Review, The Rumpus,* and elsewhere. Stacey holds an MFA from Fresno State and teaches creative writing online at The Poetry Barn and The Loft. www.staceybalkun.com

**Cathy Barber**'s work has appeared in many publications including *Sweet, SLAB, Concho River Review, Tattoo Highway,* and the ecological anthology *Fire and Rain: Ecopoetry of California.* Her poetry was nominated for a Best of the Net award in 2016. Her chapbook, *Aardvarks, Bloodhounds, Catfish, Dingoes,* was published in 2018 (Dancing Girl Press). She has an MA in English from California State University, Hayward, and an MFA in poetry from the Vermont College of Fine Arts. She makes her home in Cleveland Heights, Ohio.

**Tony Barnstone** teaches at Whittier College and is the author of 20 books and a music CD. His books of poetry include *Pulp Sonnets; Beast in the Apartment; Tongue of War: From Pearl Harbor to Nagasaki; The Golem of Los Angeles; Sad Jazz: Sonnets; Impure;* and the bilingual *Buddha in Flames: Selected Poems/Buda en Llamas: Antología poética (1999–2012).* He is also a distinguished translator of Chinese literature. His awards include the Poets Prize, Strokestown International Prize, Pushcart Prize in Poetry, John Ciardi Prize, Benjamin Saltman Award, and fellowships from the NEA, NEH, and California Arts Council.

**Grace Bauer** has published five books of poems—most recently *MEAN/TIME* (University of New Mexico Press) and a 25th anniversary reissue of *The Women at the Well* (Stephen F. Austin State University Press). She is also coeditor of the anthology *Nasty Women Poets: An Unapologetic Anthology of Subversive Verse.*

**Brian Baumgart** is the author of *Rules for Loving Right* (Sweet), and his writing has appeared in a number of journals, including *South Dakota Review, Cleaver, Whale Road Review,* and *Midway Journal.* He is the director of creative writing at North Hennepin Community College in Brooklyn Park, Minnesota, where he also curates the Meet the Authors Reading Series. In 2018, Baumgart was artist-in-residence at University of Minnesota's Cedar Creek Ecological Science Reserve, where he began working on a manuscript exploring the convergence of art, humanity, and science. https://briandbaumgart.wixsite.com/website

**Jack B. Bedell** is professor of English and coordinator of creative writing at Southeastern Louisiana University where he also edits Louisiana Literature and directs the Louisiana Literature Press. His latest collection is *No Brother, This Storm* (Mercer University Press). He served as Louisiana Poet Laureate 2017–2019.

**Kimberly Blaeser**, writer, photographer, and scholar, served as Wisconsin Poet Laureate for 2015–16. She is the author of four poetry collections—most recently *Copper Yearning* and *Apprenticed to Justice*; and editor of *Traces in Blood, Bone, and Stone: Contemporary Ojibwe Poetry*. Anishinaabe from White Earth Reservation, Blaeser is a professor at University of Wisconsin–Milwaukee and MFA faculty member for the Institute of American Indian Arts in Santa Fe. She lives in Lyons Township, Wisconsin, and, for portions of each year, in a water-access cabin near the Boundary Waters Canoe Area Wilderness where she chases poems, photos, and river otters—sometimes all at once.

**Janet Bowdan** is the author of the chapbook *Making Progress* (Finishing Line Press). Her poems have been published in many journals, including *APR*, *Denver Quarterly*, *Coffee Poems Anthology*, and *Hobart*. She teaches at Western New England University. She lives in Northampton, Massachusetts, with her husband, son, and stepdaughter.

**Elizabeth Bradfield** is the author of *Once Removed, Approaching Ice, Interpretive Work*, and *Toward Antarctica*, which combines her photographs with brief hybrid essays. *Theorem*, a collaboration with artist Antonia Contro, is forthcoming in fall 2020. Her work has been published in *The New Yorker*, *Kenyon Review*, and elsewhere. Founder and editor-in-chief of Broadsided Press, she works as a naturalist/guide and teaches creative writing at Brandeis University. www.ebradfield.com

**Fleda Brown** is the author of ten poetry collections, most recently *The Woods Are On Fire* (University of Nebraska Press). Her work has won the Felix Pollak Prize, a Pushcart Prize, the Philip Levine Prize, and the Great Lakes Colleges New Writer's Award, and has twice been a finalist for the National Poetry Series. She lives in Traverse City, Michigan, and is on the faculty of the Rainier Writing Workshop, a low-residency MFA program in Tacoma, Washington.

**Sarah Carey** is a graduate of the Florida State University creative writing program. She is the author of two poetry chapbooks, *The Heart Contracts* (Finishing Line) and *Accommodations*, winner of the 2018 Concrete Wolf Chapbook Award. A Pushcart and Orison prize nominee, her poems have recently appeared in or are forthcoming from *Grist, Stirring, Frontier Poetry, Split Rock Review, SWWIM Every Day, Atticus Review*, and elsewhere. She works in communications at the University of Florida and lives in Gainesville.

**Judith Chalmer** is the author of two collections of poems, *Minnow* (Kelsay Books) and *Out of History's Junk Jar* (Time Being Books). She is co-translator of two books of haiku and tanka with Michiko Oishi, *Red Fish Alphabet* (Honami Syoten) and *Deepening Snow* (Plowboy Press). Before retiring, she was director of VSA Vermont, now Inclusive Arts Vermont, a nonprofit in arts and disability, for which she received the 2018 Arthur Williams Award from the Vermont Arts Council for Meritorious Service in the Arts. She lives with her partner, Lisa, in Vermont.

**Robin Chapman**'s ten poetry collections include *Abundance*, recipient of Cider Press Editors' Book Award, which includes poems of the Boundary Waters, and books focused on species loss (*the eelgrass meadow*), climate change (*One Hundred White Pelicans*), and growing up in the Manhattan Project town of Oak Ridge, Tennessee (*Six True Things*). *The Only Home We Know* is her most recent book, and her poems have recently appeared in *The Hudson Review*, *Alaska Quarterly Review*, and *Valparaiso Poetry Review*. She is the recipient of the 2010 Appalachia Poetry Prize.

**Paula Cisewski**'s fourth poetry collection, *Quitter*, won the Diode Editions Book Prize. She is also the author of *The Threatened Everything* and *Ghost Fargo*, winner of the Nightboat Poetry Prize, selected by Franz Wright, as well as several chapbooks, including the lyric prose *Misplaced Sinister*. She has been awarded fellowships and residencies from the Jerome Foundation, Minnesota State Arts Board, Oberholtzer Foundation, Banfill-Locke Center for the Arts, and House of Helsinglight. Cisewski lives in Minneapolis, where she teaches, collaborates with fellow artists and activists, and serves on the editorial staff of *Conduit*.

**Patricia Clark** is the author of five volumes of poetry, including *The Canopy* (Terrapin Books) and *Sunday Rising* (Michigan State University Press). She has also published three chapbooks: *Wreath for the Red Admiral, Given the Trees,* and most recently *Deadlifts* (New Michigan Press). From 2005 to 2007 she was honored to serve as the poet laureate of Grand Rapids, Michigan. She is poet-in-residence and a professor in the Department of Writing at Grand Valley State University in Michigan.

**Sudasi J. Clement** has lived on the East Coast, the West Coast, and for nearly 30 years in the high desert of New Mexico. She is the author of the chapbook *The Bones We Have in Common* (Slipstream Press) and is the former poetry editor of *Santa Fe Literary Review* (2006–2016). Sudasi's poems have appeared in *Apalachee Review, Sierra Nevada Review, Room Magazine, Nerve Cowboy, The Mas Tequila Review,* and *Ovunque Siamo,* among others. She and her wife are proprietors of a bustling mom-and-mom shop, Beadweaver of Santa Fe.

**Susan Cohen** is the author of *Throat Singing* and *A Different Wakeful Animal,* winner of the David Martinson-Meadowhawk Prize from Red Dragonfly Press. Her poems have appeared in *Nimrod, Poet Lore, Prairie Schooner, Southern Humanities Review, Southern Review, Valparaiso Poetry Review,* and many other journals and anthologies, including: *Atlanta Review 25th Anniversary Anthology; Bloomsbury Anthology of Contemporary Jewish American Poetry; Fire and Rain, Eco-poetry of California;* and *America We Call Your Name, Poems of Resistance and Resilience.* She lives in California and has an MFA from Pacific University.

**Anne Coray** lives at her birthplace in remote southwest Alaska. Her debut novel, *Lost Mountain,* is forthcoming in 2021 from West Margin Press. She is also the author of three poetry collections: *Bone Strings, A Measure's Hush,* and *Violet Transparent;* and coeditor of *Crosscurrents North: Alaskans on the Environment* (University of Alaska Press). Her work has appeared in many literary journals, including the *Southern Review, Northwest Review, North American Review,* and *AQR.* Coray is the recipient of fellowships from the Alaska State Council on the Arts and the Rasmuson Foundation.

**James Crews** is the author of two full-length collections of poetry, *The Book of What Stays* and *Telling My Father.* He is also the editor of *Healing the Divide: Poems of Kindness and Connection,* published by Green Writers Press, and lives on part of an organic farm with his husband in Shaftsbury, Vermont. He leads mindfulness and writing workshops throughout the country.

**Todd Davis** is the author of six full-length collections of poetry, most recently *Native Species*, *Winterkill*, and *In the Kingdom of the Ditch*, all published by Michigan State University Press. He has won the Foreword INDIES Book of the Year bronze and silver awards, the Gwendolyn Brooks Poetry Prize, and the Chautauqua Editors Prize. His poems appear in such noted journals and magazines as *Alaska Quarterly Review*, *American Poetry Review*, *Barrow Street*, *Gettysburg Review*, *Iowa Review*, *Missouri Review*, *North American Review*, *Orion*, and *Poetry Northwest*. He teaches environmental studies at Pennsylvania State University's Altoona College.

**Rosemarie Dombrowski** is the inaugural poet laureate of Phoenix, Arizona, and the founding editor of rinky dink press and *The Revolution (Relaunch)*. She's the recipient of five Pushcart nominations, an Arts Hero Award, a Women & Philanthropy grant, and a fellowship from the Lincoln Center for Applied Ethics. Dombrowski has published three collections of poetry to date, including *The Cleavage Planes of Southwest Minerals [A Love Story]*, winner of the 2017 *Split Rock Review* chapbook competition. www.rdpoet.com

**Lynn Domina** is the author of two collections of poetry, *Corporal Works* and *Framed in Silence,* and the editor of a collection of essays, *Poets on the Psalms.* Her recent work appears in many periodicals and anthologies. She serves as creative writing editor for *The Other Journal* and as head of the English Department at Northern Michigan University. www.lynndomina.com

**Eileen Walsh Duncan**'s poems have appeared in numerous journals, including *Cascadia Review*, *Crab Creek Review*, *Fault Lines Journal*, *Hubbub*, *Off the Coast*, *Seattle Review*, *Pontoon*, *Pure Francis*, and *The Washington State Geospatial Poetry Anthology*. She received the Bentley Award from *Seattle Review* and has been nominated for the Pushcart Prize.

**Camille T. Dungy** is the author of *Guidebook to Relative Strangers: Journeys into Race, Motherhood, and History*, *Trophic Cascade*, *Smith Blue*, and *Suck on the Marrow*, among others. She edited *Black Nature: Four Centuries of African American Nature Poetry* and coedited the *From the Fishouse* poetry anthology. Her honors include an American Book Award, two Northern California Book Awards, a California Book Award silver medal, and a fellowship from the NEA. Dungy is currently a professor in the English Department at Colorado State University.

**Alan Elyshevitz** is the author of a collection of stories, *The Widows and Orphans Fund* (SFA Press), and three poetry chapbooks, most recently *Imaginary Planet* (Cervena Barva). His poems have appeared in *River Styx*, *Nimrod International Journal*, and *Water~Stone Review*, among others. Winner of the *North American Review* James Hearst Poetry Prize, he is also a two-time recipient of a fellowship in fiction writing from the Pennsylvania Council on the Arts. https://aelyshevitz.ink

**Michelle Bonczek Evory** is the author of *The Ghosts of Lost Animals*, winner of the 2018 Barry Spacks Poetry Prize from Gunpowder Press, three poetry chapbooks, and the Open SUNY Textbook *Naming the Unnamable: An Approach to Poetry for New Generations*. Her poetry is featured in the *Best New Poets Anthology*, *Crazyhorse*, *cream city review*, *Green Mountains Review*, *Orion*, *The Progressive*, *Wasifiri: International Contemporary Writing*, and elsewhere. She holds an MFA from Eastern Washington University and a PhD from Western Michigan University. She mentors poets at The Poet's Billow. www.thepoetsbillow.org

**Jeff Fearnside** is the author of *Making Love While Levitating Three Feet in the Air* (Stephen F. Austin State University Press). His poetry, fiction, and nonfiction have appeared in numerous journals and anthologies, including *The Paris Review*, *The Los Angeles Review*, *The Pinch*, *Story*, *Permafrost*, *Rosebud Magazine*, and *Forest Under Story: Creative Inquiry in an Old-Growth Forest* (University of Washington Press). Honors for his work include a Grand Prize in the Santa Fe Writers Project's Literary Awards Program, a Peace Corps Writers Poetry Award, and an Oregon Arts Commission Individual Artist Fellowship. He teaches at Oregon State University.

**Michael Garrigan** writes and teaches along the banks of the Susquehanna River in Pennsylvania. He enjoys exploring the river's tributaries with a fly rod and hiking the riverlands, and feels strongly that every watershed should have a poet laureate. Garrigan is the author of the chapbook *What I Know [How to Do]* (Finishing Line Press) and a full-length poetry collection, *Robbing the Pillars* (Homebound Publications). His writing has appeared in *Gray's Sporting Journal*, *The Wayfarer*, *The Drake Magazine*, *Permafrost*, *Sky Island Journal*, and *Split Rock Review*. www.mgarrigan.com

**Ginnie Goulet Gavrin** worked as a massage therapist for more than 25 years. Currently, she teaches meditation and writing workshops at the Monadnock Mindfulness Practice Center in Keene, New Hampshire. She holds a master of fine arts degree from the Stonecoast MFA in Creative Writing. Her poetry has appeared in *The Literary Review, The Worcester Review, THEMA, Primavera, Slipstream, Oyster River Pages, Leaping Clear, The Greensboro Review,* and the anthology, *Essential Love: Poems About Mothers and Fathers, Daughters and Sons.*

**Louise Glück** is the author of a dozen poetry collections and *American Originality: Essays on Poetry.* Her awards include the National Book Award, the Pulitzer Prize, the National Book Critics Circle Award, the Bollingen Prize for Poetry, and the Wallace Stevens Award from the Academy of American Poets. She teaches at Yale University and lives in Cambridge, Massachusetts.

**Benjamin Goluboff** teaches English at Lake Forest College. In addition to publishing articles in some scholarly publications, he has published poetry, fiction, and essays in many small-press journals over the years. He is the author of *Ho Chi Minh: A Speculative Life in Verse* and *Biking Englewood: An Essay on the White Gaze,* both from Urban Farmhouse Press.

**Jeffrey Greene** has published five collections of poetry and a book of mixed-genre writing. He is the author of the memoir *French Spirits* and three personalized nature books. His writing has been supported by the National Endowment for the Arts, Connecticut Commission on the Arts, and the Rinehart Fund, and he was a winner of the Samuel French Morse Prize, the Randall Jarrell Award, and the Discovery/The Nation Award. His writing has appeared numerous publications, including *The New Yorker, Poetry, The Nation, Ploughshares,* and *Agni* as well as many anthologies.

**Tresha Faye Haefner** poetry has appeared in or is forthcoming from *Blood Lotus, The Cincinnati Review, Hunger Mountain, Pirene's Fountain, Poet Lore, Prairie Schooner, Radar, Rattle,* and *TinderBox.* Her work has garnered several accolades, including the 2011 Robert and Adele Schiff Poetry Prize, and a 2012 nomination for a Pushcart.

**Joy Harjo**, the 23rd poet laureate of the United States, is a member of the Mvskoke Nation and belongs to Oce Vpofv (Hickory Ground). Harjo is the author of nine books of poetry, including *An American Sunrise* and *Conflict Resolution for Holy Beings*. Her awards for poetry include the Ruth Lily Prize for Lifetime Achievement, the Academy of American Poets Wallace Stevens Award, the New Mexico Governor's Award for Excellence in the Arts, a PEN USA Literary Award, Lila Wallace-Reader's Digest Fund Writers' Award, a Rasmuson US Artist Fellowship, two NEA fellowships, and a Guggenheim Fellowship. www.joyharjo.com

**Andrew Hemmert**'s poems have appeared in or are forthcoming from *Barrow Street*, *Iron Horse Literary Review*, *The Journal*, *North American Review*, and *Washington Square Review*. He won the 2018 River Styx International Poetry Contest. He earned his MFA from Southern Illinois University, Carbondale, and currently lives in Colorado Springs.

**Elise Hempel** is the author of *Second Rain* (Able Muse Press). Her poems have appeared in numerous journals over the years, as well as in *Poetry Daily* and *American Life in Poetry*. She is the recipient of an Illinois Arts Council Literary Award and the winner of the 2015 Able Muse Write Prize in Poetry, the 2016 String Poet Prize, and the 2017 No Chair Press Chapbook Contest. Hempel lives in central Illinois but has a lifelong connection with northern Wisconsin, and most of her family now lives in Minnesota.

**Michael Hettich** is the author of several poetry collections, including *To Start an Orchard* (Press 53), *Bluer and More Vast* (Hysterical Books), *The Frozen Harbor* (Red Dragonfly Press), and *Systems of Vanishing* (University of Tampa Press). His work has appeared widely in journals. A long-time resident of Miami, he moved to Black Mountain, North Carolina, in 2018. www.michaelhettich.com

**Gwendolyn Ann Hill**, originally from Iowa City, Iowa, received an Academy of American Poets Prize, as well as awards and fellowships from the University of Arkansas, where she is finishing up her MFA. Her writing has been supported by the Bread Loaf Environmental Writers' Conference, and her poems have appeared in or are forthcoming from *Poets.org*, *Prairie Schooner*, *Painted Bride Quarterly*, and others. She develops environmental writing workshops with the Open Mouth Reading Series, serving as their educational director, and lives in Fayetteville, Arkansas. www.gwendolynannhill.com

**Sean Hill** is the author of two poetry collections, *Dangerous Goods* (Milkweed Editions) and *Blood Ties & Brown Liquor* (UGA Press). He has received numerous awards including fellowships from the Cave Canem Foundation, Stanford University, and the National Endowment for the Arts. His poems and essays have appeared in or are forthcoming from *Callaloo*, *Harvard Review*, *New England Review*, *Oxford American*, *Poetry*, *Terrain.org*, *Tin House*, and numerous other journals, and in over a dozen anthologies, including *Black Nature* and *Villanelles*. He directs the Minnesota Northwoods Writers Conference at Bemidji State University and lives in Montana. www.seanhillpoetry.com

**Marybeth Holleman** is the author of *The Heart of the Sound* and *Among Wolves*, and coeditor of *Crosscurrents North*. Her first poetry collection, *tender gravity*, is forthcoming from Red Hen Press. Pushcart-prize nominee and finalist for the Siskiyou Prize, she's published in venues including *Orion*, *Christian Science Monitor*, *Sierra*, *Literary Mama*, *ISLE/OUP*, *North American Review*, *AQR*, *zoomorphic*, *Minding Nature*, *The Guardian*, *The Future of Nature*, and on NPR. Raised in North Carolina's Smokies, Holleman transplanted to Alaska's Chugach Mountains after falling head over heels for Prince William Sound just two years before the EVOS oil spill. www.marybethholleman.com

**Bethany Schultz Hurst** is the author of *Miss Lost Nation*, winner of the Anhinga Poetry Prize, and finalist for the 2016 Kate Tufts Discovery Award. Her work has appeared in *Best American Poetry 2015* and in journals such as *Ecotone*, *The Gettysburg Review*, *Gulf Coast*, *Narrative*, and *Ploughshares*. A recent recipient of a literary arts fellowship through the Idaho Commission on the Arts, she is an associate professor at Idaho State University.

**Jim Johnson**, a former Duluth poet laureate, lived most of his life in northern Minnesota where he developed an awareness and concern for local culture and history, as well as for the natural world. He has published ten books of poetry, most recently *One Morning in June: Selected Poems* (Red Dragonfly Press). He now lives in Cedar Falls, Iowa, and Isabella, Minnesota.

**Jen Karetnick** is the author of ten poetry collections, including *Let's Swan Sing* (Salmon Poetry, forthcoming 2023); *The Burning Where Breath Used to Be* (David Robert Books); and *The Crossing Over*, winner of the 2018 *Split Rock Review* Chapbook Competition. Her poems have been awarded the Hart Crane Memorial Prize, the Romeo Lemay Poetry Prize, the Anna Davidson Rosenberg Prize, and two Dorothy Sargent Rosenberg Prizes, among others. Her work appears in *Barrow Street*, *The Comstock Review*, *december*, *Michigan Quarterly Review*, *Terrain.org*, and elsewhere. Karetnick is cofounder and managing editor of *SWWIM Every Day*. www.jkaretnick.com

**Julia Spicher Kasdorf** is the author of four books of poetry, including *Shale Play: Poems and Photographs from the Fracking Fields*. Her awards include the Agnes Lynch Starrett Poetry Prize, Great Lakes College's Association Award for New Writing, a Pushcart Prize, and a National Endowment for the Arts Fellowship in Poetry. She is professor of English and women's, gender, and sexuality studies at Penn State, where she teaches creative writing. www.juliakasdorf.com

**Jayne Fenton Keane** is an award-winning, extensively published poet whose plays, poetry collections, websites, CDs, performances, and academic articles have been widely recognized. Nominated for the Pushcart Prize three times, she was shortlisted for the Griffith University Medal for her doctorate, *Three Dimensional Poetic Natures*. Her radio play *A Night with no Explanation* was nominated by the ABC for the 2010 Prix Italia, and she has been a guest of leading global literature festivals. She enjoys collaboration.

**Benjamín Naka-Hasebe Kingsley** is a recipient of the Provincetown Fine Arts Work Center and Tickner Fellowships. He belongs to the Onondaga Nation of Indigenous Americans in New York. His work appears in *Poetry*, *Poets.org*, *Field*, *The Georgia Review*, *jubilat*, *Kenyon Review*, *Missouri Review*, *New England Review*, *Oxford American*, and *Tin House*, among others.

**Jacqueline Kolosov** is the author of three poetry collections, including *Memory of Blue* (Salmon Poetry). Her poems, stories, essays, and hybrid work have appeared in journals such as *Orion, Poetry,* and *The Sewanee Review.* In 2008, she received an NEA Literature Fellowship in prose. You can find her craft essays, along with interviews and reviews, in places like *The Writer's Chronicle* and *The Georgia Review.* She lives in Texas.

**Ted Kooser** won the Pulitzer Prize for his poetry collection, *Delights & Shadows* from Copper Canyon Press. His next collection is *Red Stilts,* due out in the fall of 2020, also from Copper Canyon. His most recent picture book for children is *Mr. Posey's New Glasses* from Candlewick Press.

**Lance Larsen** is the author of five poetry collections, most recently *What the Body Knows* (Tampa, 2018). He has received a Pushcart Prize and fellowships from Ragdale, Sewanee, and the National Endowment for the Arts. Six of his nonfiction pieces have been listed as notables in Best American Essays. Larsen was Utah's poet laureate from 2012 to 2017. He teaches at BYU, where he serves as department chair.

**Mercedes Lawry** is the author of *Small Measures,* forthcoming from Twelve Winters Press, and three chapbooks, the latest of which, *In the Early Garden with Reason,* was selected by Molly Peacock for the 2018 WaterSedge Chapbook Contest. Her poetry has appeared in several journals, including *Poetry, Nimrod,* and *Prairie Schooner.* Lawry's work has been nominated five times for a Pushcart Prize, and her fiction was a semifinalist in the Best Small Fictions 2016. Additionally, she's published stories and poems for children. She lives in Seattle.

**Ada Limón** is the author of five books of poetry, including *The Carrying,* which won the National Book Critics Circle Award for Poetry. Her fourth book, *Bright Dead Things,* was named a finalist for the National Book Award, a finalist for the Kingsley Tufts Poetry Award, and a finalist for the National Book Critics Circle Award. She serves on the faculty of Queens University of Charlotte Low Residency MFA program and the online and summer programs for the Provincetown Fine Arts Work Center.

**D.A. Lockhart** is the author of *Devil in the Woods* (Brick Books) and *Wenchikaneit Visions* (Black Moss). His work has appeared widely throughout Turtle Island, including Best Canadian Poetry 2019, *Malahat Review*, *Grain*, *CV2*, *TriQuarterly*, *The Fiddlehead*, and *Belt*. He is pùkuwànkoamimëns of the Moravian of the Thames First Nation. Lockhart currently resides at Waawiiyaatanong where he is the publisher at Urban Farmhouse Press and poetry editor at the *Windsor Review*.

**Debra Marquart** is the author of several books, including *Small Buried Things* and *The Horizontal World: Growing up Wild in the Middle of Nowhere*. She teaches in the MFA Program in Creative Writing and Environment at Iowa State University and the Stonecoast Low-Residency MFA Program at University of Southern Maine. In 2019 Marquart was named Iowa's poet laureate.

**Anne Haven McDonnell** lives in Santa Fe, New Mexico, and teaches as an associate professor at the Institute of American Indian Arts. Her work has been published in *Orion, The Georgia Review, The American Journal of Poetry, Nimrod, Terrain.org*, and elsewhere. Her work won the fifth annual *Terrain.org* poetry prize and second place for the international ecopoetry Gingko prize. Her chapbook, *Living with Wolves*, will be out with Split Rock Press in 2020. Anne has been a writer-in-residence at the Andrews Forest Writers' Residency and the Sitka Center for Art and Ecology.

**Amy Miller**'s full-length poetry collection *The Trouble with New England Girls* won the Louis Award from Concrete Wolf Press. Her writing has appeared in *Barrow Street, Gulf Coast, Nimrod, Rattle, Tupelo Quarterly, Willow Springs*, and *ZYZZYVA*. She lives in Ashland, Oregon, where she works as the publications manager for the Oregon Shakespeare Festival.

**Leslie Adrienne Miller**'s collections of poetry include *Y, The Resurrection Trade*, and *Eat Quite Everything You See* (Graywolf Press), and *Yesterday Had a Man In It, Ungodliness*, and *Staying Up For Love* (Carnegie Mellon University Press). Miller's poems have appeared in *Best American Poetry, American Poetry Review, Antioch Review, Harvard Review, Georgia Review, Ploughshares,* and *Crazyhorse*. Professor of English at the University of St. Thomas, she holds degrees in creative writing and literature from Stephens College, University of Missouri, Iowa Writers Workshop, and University of Houston. www.lesliemillerpoet.com

**Felicia Mitchell** makes her home in the mountains of southwest Virginia. Her poems about the natural world have appeared widely, including in *Terrain.org* and *Mountains Piled Upon Mountains: Appalachian Nature Writing in the Anthropocene* (edited by Jessica Cory for West Virginia University Press). Her recent collection of poetry is *Waltzing with Horses* (Press 53). www.feliciamitchell.net

**Sarah Fawn Montgomery** is the author of *Quite Mad: An American Pharma Memoir* (Ohio State University Press) and the poetry chapbooks *Regenerate: Poems of Mad Women, Leaving Tracks: A Prairie Guide*, and *The Astronaut Checks His Watch*. She is an assistant professor at Bridgewater State University.

**Juan J. Morales** is the author of three poetry collections, including *The Handyman's Guide to End Times* (University of New Mexico Press), winner of the 2019 International Latino Book Award. He is a CantoMundo Fellow, editor of *Pilgrimage Magazine*, and a Professor and the Department Chair of English and World Languages at Colorado State University-Pueblo.

**Rachel Morgan** is the author of the chapbook, *Honey & Blood, Blood & Honey* (Final Thursday Press), and she is the coeditor of *Fire Under the Moon: An Anthology of Contemporary Slovene Poetry* (Black Dirt Press). Her work recently appeared in the anthology *Fracture: Essays, Poems, and Stories on Fracking in America* (Ice Cube Press) and in *Alaska Quarterly Review, Barrow Street, Boulevard, Crazyhorse, Prairie Schooner, Salt Hill, Split Rock Review*, and elsewhere. She was a finalist for the 2017 National Poetry Series. Currently, she teaches at the University of Northern Iowa and is the poetry editor for *North American Review*.

**Shelby Newsom** is the associate editor for Autumn House Press and a fact checker for Creative Nonfiction Foundation. She received her MFA in poetry from Chatham University. Her work has been nominated for Pushcart and Best New Poets and is featured in *The Hopper, Flyway: Journal of Writing and Environment, Pilgrimage Magazine, Deep Wild*, and *Hawk & Whippoorwill*. She lives in Pittsburgh, Pennsylvania. www.shelbynewsom.com

**Aimee Nezhukumatathil** is the author of four poetry collections and a book of illustrated nature essays, *World of Wonders: In Praise of Fireflies, Whale Sharks, & Other Astonishments,* (Milkweed Editions). She is the poetry editor of *Orion* and her poems have appeared in *American Poetry Review, New England Review, Poetry, Ploughshares, Tin House,* among others. Honors include a poetry fellowship from the National Endowment for the Arts and the Pushcart Prize. She is professor of English in the University of Mississippi's MFA program.

**Greg Nicholl** is a freelance editor whose poetry has recently appeared in or is forthcoming from *Crab Orchard Review, Ecotone, Mid-American Review, Nimrod, North American Review, Post Road, Prairie Schooner,* and elsewhere. He is a four-time Pushcart Prize nominee and currently lives in Boston.

**Ed O'Casey** studied at the University of North Texas and New Mexico State University. He is the author of *Proximidad: A Mexican/American Memoir* and various other transformations that have appeared in or are upcoming from *Berkeley Poetry Review, Cold Mountain Review, Euphony, Split Rock Review, Tulane Review, Poetry Quarterly, Whiskey Island,* and *NANO Fiction.* He lives in San Antonio, Texas.

**Sharon Olds** is the author of numerous books of poetry. *Stag's Leap* received the T.S. Eliot Prize and the Pulitzer Prize; *The Dead and the Living* received the National Book Critics Circle Award; and *The Unswept Room* was a finalist for the National Book Award and the National Book Critics Circle Award. From 1998 to 2000, she was the New York State poet laureate. She teaches creative writing at New York University.

**C. Mikal Oness** is the author of *Oracle Bones* (Lewis-Clark Press) and *Water Becomes Bone* (New Issues Press) and winner of the Lewis & Clark Poetry Prize. He is the founding editor of Sutton Hoo Press, a literary fine press, and lives on a cottage farm in Southeastern Minnesota with his wife, Elizabeth Oness.

**Elizabeth Oness** is the author of *Articles of Faith, Departures, Twelve Rivers of the Body, Fallibility,* and *Leaving Milan.* Her poems and stories have appeared in *The Georgia Review, The Gettysburg Review, Glimmer Train, The Hudson Review, The Tahoma Literary Review,* and other magazines. Her stories have received an O. Henry Prize, a Nelson Algren Award, and the Crazyhorse Fiction Prize. She directs marketing and development for Sutton Hoo Press, a literary fine press, and is a professor of English at Winona State University.

**Sheila Packa** is the author of four poetry books and was a former poet laureate of Duluth, Minnesota. She teaches writing in the community and is at work on a new manuscript about water, the northern Minnesota landscape, and displacements. Recently, her poems were set into a musical composition in *Sibelius: Kullervo & Kortekangas: Migrations* performed by the Minnesota Orchestra and recorded by BIS.

**Craig Santos Perez** is an indigenous Pacific Islander poet from Guam. He is the author of four books of poetry and the editor of four anthologies. He teaches environmental poetry and creative writing at the University of Hawai'i, Manoa.

**Vivian Faith Prescott** was born and raised in southeast Alaska and lives at her family's fish camp—Mickey's Fishcamp—in Wrangell, Alaska. She holds an MFA from the University of Alaska and a PhD in cross-cultural studies from the University of Alaska, Fairbanks. She's a two-time recipient of a Rasmuson Individual Artist Award. She's also the author of four chapbooks, two full-length poetry books, and a short story collection. Along with her daughter, Vivian Mork Yéilk', she writes a column for the *Juneau Empire* called "Planet Alaska."

**Kimberly Ann Priest** is the author of *Still Life* (PANK), *Parrot Flower* (Glass Poetry Press), and *White Goat Black Sheep* (FLP). She is a winner of a 2019 Heartland Poetry Prize from New American Press, and her work has appeared in several journals, including *The Laurel Review, The Berkeley Poetry Review,* and *riverSedge.* A graduate of the MFA program at New England College, she is currently an assistant professor at Michigan State University and serves as a poetry editor for the *Nimrod International Journal of Prose and Poetry.* www.kimberlyannpriest.com

**Mary Quade** is the author of the poetry collections *Guide to Native Beasts* (Cleveland State University) and *Local Extinctions* (Gold Wake). She is the recipient of an Oregon Literary Fellowship and three Ohio Arts Council Individual Excellence Awards in both poetry and creative nonfiction. She spent her childhood in Wisconsin and now lives in northeast Ohio, where she teaches creative writing at Hiram College.

**Kathleen Radigan** holds a BA from Wesleyan University and an MFA from Boston University. Her work appears in *Carve, New Ohio Review, Antigonish Review*, Belladonna Series, and the Academy of American Poets, among others. Her chapbook, *The Frustrated Ones*, is forthcoming from dancing girl press. Radigan received an Olin Fellowship from Wesleyan to study banshees and other ghosts in Ireland and a Robert Pinsky Global Fellowship in Poetry for travel to Italy. She was recently named a Brooklyn Poets Fellow. She teaches writing to public high school students in New York.

**Quinn Rennerfeldt** studied creative writing at the University of Colorado at Boulder and currently lives in San Francisco with her family and animal menagerie. Her heart is equally wed to the Pacific Ocean and the Rocky Mountains. Her work can be found in *Slipstream, Bird's Thumb, SAND*, Punch Drunk Press, and elsewhere. She is the cofounder of *Q/A Poetry*, a journal promoting womxn and nonbinary poets.

**Karen Rigby** is the author of *Chinoiserie* (Ahsahta Press). Her poems have been published in *Australian Book Review, The London Magazine, The Spectacle*, and other journals. She lives in Arizona. www.karenrigby.com

**Sara Ryan** is the author of the chapbooks *Never Leave the Foot of an Animal Unskinned* (Porkbelly Press) and *Excellent Evidence of Human Activity* (Cupboard Pamphlet). In 2018, she won *Grist*'s Pro Forma Contest and *Cutbank*'s Big Sky, Small Prose Contest. Her work has been published in or is forthcoming from *Pleiades, DIAGRAM, Redivider, Prairie Schooner, Thrush Poetry Journal*, and others. She is an associate editor for both *Iron Horse Literary Review* and *Split Lip Magazine*. She is currently pursuing her PhD at Texas Tech University.

**Marjorie Saiser**'s new book, *Learning to Swim* (Stephen F. Austin State University Press), combines poetry and memoir. Her work has been nominated for a Pushcart Prize and has been published in or is forthcoming from *Rattle*, *Alaska Quarterly Review*, *I-70 Review*, *Briar Cliff Review*, *bosque*, *Water-Stone Review*, and *American Life in Poetry*. www.poetmarge.com

**Cintia Santana** is a poet and interdisciplinary artist. The recipient of fellowships from CantoMundo and the Djerassi Resident Artists Program, she currently teaches poetry and fiction workshops in Spanish as well as literary translation courses at Stanford University.

**Kathryn Savage** is a hybrid writer whose debut lyric essay collection, *Groundglass*, is forthcoming from Coffee House Press. Her writing appears in *American Short Fiction*, *Guardian*, *BOMB Magazine*, *Academy of American Poets poets.org*, and *The Beloit Fiction Journal*, among others. A recipient of the 2018 Academy of American Poets James Wright Prize, she's a current Tulsa Artist Fellow.

**James Scruton** is the author of two full collections and five chapbooks of poems, including *Crossing the Days* (Prolific Press) and *The Rules* (Green Linden Press), both published in 2019. The recipient of the Frederick Bock Prize from *Poetry* magazine as well as the Finishing Line Press Poetry Prize and the Grayson Books Poetry Award, he is currently a professor of English and associate academic dean at Bethel University in McKenzie, Tennessee.

**M. Bartley Seigel** is the author of *This Is What They Say* (Typecast Publishing); founding editor emeritus of *PANK Magazine*; and associate professor of creative writing at Michigan Technological University. His poetry appears in journals such as *DIAGRAM*, *Fourth River*, *Michigan Quarterly Review*, *Split Rock Review*, and *Thrush*, among others, and was most recently anthologized in *And Here: 100 Years of Upper Peninsula Writing* (Michigan State University Press). He lives in Houghton, Ojibwe and Treaty of 1842 territory, Michigan.

**Martha Silano** is the author of five poetry books, including *Gravity Assist*, *The Little Office of the Immaculate Conception*, and *Reckless Lovely*, all from Saturnalia Books. She also coauthored, with Kelli Russell Agodon, *The Daily Poet: Day-By-Day Prompts for Your Writing Practice*. Her poems have appeared in *Paris Review*, *Poetry*, *New England Review*, and *American Poetry Review*, among others. Silano teaches at Bellevue College, near her home in Seattle, Washington.

**Alessandra Simmons** is an English PhD candidate at University of Wisconsin–Milwaukee and a flower farmer on Washington Island. She has poems published in *Spillway* (nominated for a Pushcart Prize), *Aquifer: Florida Review Online*, *Rabbit Catastrophe*, and other journals. She helps run Gathering Ground, an educational agricultural nonprofit.

**Karen Skolfield**'s book *Battle Dress* (W. W. Norton) won the Barnard Women Poets Prize. Her book *Frost in the Low Areas* (Zone 3 Press) won the 2014 PEN New England Award in poetry, and she is the winner of the 2016 Jeffrey E. Smith Editors' Prize in poetry from *The Missouri Review*. Skolfield is a US Army veteran and teaches writing to engineers at the University of Massachusetts Amherst; she's the poet laureate for Northampton, MA for 2019–2021. www.karenskolfield.com

**Thomas R. Smith** is a poet and essayist living in River Falls, Wisconsin. The most recent of his eight books of poetry are *The Glory* (Red Dragonfly Press) and *Windy Day at Kabekona: New and Selected Prose Poems* (White Pine Press). His first prose work, *Poetry on the Side of Nature: Writing the Nature Poem as an Act of Survival*, is forthcoming from Folded Word Press. He is a longtime environmental activist and teaches poetry at the Loft Literary Center in Minneapolis.

**Karen Solie** was born in Moose Jaw, Saskatchewan. She is the author of several poetry collections, including: *The Caiplie Caves, The Road In Is Not the Same Road Out, Short Haul Engine, Modern and Normal*, and *Pigeon*, which won the Griffin Poetry Prize, the Pat Lowther Award, and the Trillium Book Award for Poetry. Solie serves as an associate director for the Banff Centre's Writing Studio program. She lives in Toronto, Ontario.

**Heidi Lynn Staples** is the author of *A\*\*A\*A\**, *Noise Event*, and *Guess Can Gallop*; winner of the New Issues Poetry Prize; and coeditor of *Poets for Living Waters* and *Big Energy Poets: When Ecopoetry Thinks Climate Change*. She serves as an assistant professor of English at the University of Alabama.

**Margo Taft Stever** is the author of several poetry collections, including *Cracked Piano* (Cavan Kerry Press) and *Ghost Moose* (Kattywompus Press). Her poems have recently appeared in *Verse Daily*, *Poem-A-Day*, *The Academy of American Poets*, *Cincinnati Review*, *Salamander*, *Prairie Schooner*, *New England Review*, and *West Branch*, among others. She is the founder of the Hudson Valley Writers Center and the founder/coeditor of Slapering Hol Press. www.margotaftstever.com

**Joyce Sutphen** grew up on a farm in Stearns County, Minnesota. She is a professor emeritus of English at Gustavus Adolphus College and is Minnesota's poet laureate. Sutphen is the author of several poetry collections, including *Carrying Water to the Field* (University of Nebraska Press), *Straight Out of View*, *Coming Back to the Body*, and *Naming the Starts*. She is coeditor of *To Sing Along the Way: Minnesota Women Poets from Pre-Territorial Days to the Present*.

**Bart Sutter** is the only writer to win the Minnesota Book Award in three different categories: poetry, fiction, and creative nonfiction. The author of nine books, Sutter's most recent collection is *Nordic Accordion: Poems in a Scandinavian Mood* (Nodin Press). He has written for public radio, he has had four verse plays produced, and he often performs as one half of the Sutter Brothers, a poetry-and-music duo. He lives in Duluth with his wife, pastel artist Dorothea Diver, on a hillside overlooking Lake Superior.

**Sharon Suzuki-Martinez's** first book, *The Way of All Flux*, won the New Rivers Press MVP Poetry Prize for 2010. She was a finalist for the 2018 Best of the Net, was awarded a residency at the Anderson Center at Tower View, and a fellowship from Kundiman, among other honors. Originally from Hawaii, she now lives in Tempe, Arizona. sharonsuzukimartinez.tumblr.com

**Heather Swan**'s poems have appeared in *Poet Lore, The Hopper, Cold Mountain Review, The Raleigh Review, Midwestern Gothic, About Place, Iris*, and *Basalt*, as well as several anthologies, including *Healing the Divide*, edited by James Crews. Her chapbook, *The Edge of Damage* (Parallel Press), won the Wisconsin Fellowship of Poets Award. Her creative nonfiction has appeared in *Aeon, Belt, ISLE, Edge Effects, Resilience Magazine*, and *Catapult* (forthcoming). Her book *Where Honeybees Thrive: Stories from the Field* won the Sigurd F. Olson Nature Writing Award, first prize at BIGNY, and the Annual New York Book Show in 2018.

**Meredith Trede** is the author of *Field Theory* (Stephen F. Austin State University Press), *Out of the Book*, and *Tenement Threnody* (Main Street Rag Press), persona poems in voices from her city childhood. A Toadlily Press founder, her journal publications include *Barrow Street, Cortland Review, Friends Journal, Witness*, and *Paris Review*. She was granted fellowships at Blue Mountain Center, Ragdale, Saltonstall, and the Virginia Center for the Creative Arts. She serves on the Slapering Hol Press Advisory Committee.

**Jessica Turcat** teaches for the Gender and Women's Studies Program at Oklahoma State University. Her work has appeared in *San Diego Poetry Annual, Indiana Review, American Literary Review, Aesthetica, Magma Poetry, Reed Magazine, Spillway, So to Speak*, and *MuseWrite's Shifts: An Anthology of Women's Growth Through Change*, among others. She was the recipient of the 2015 Writers@Work fellowship for poetry, the 2013 Rash Awards, and the 2013 Edwin Markham Prize for Poetry.

**Ryan Vine** is the author of *To Keep Him Hidden* (Salmon Poetry), winner of the 2018 Northeastern Minnesota Book Award for poetry. His chapbook, *Distant Engines*, won a Weldon Kees Award in 2005 from the Backwaters Press. Vine's poems have appeared in *The American Poetry Review, Ploughshares, Poetry Ireland Review, Poetry Daily*, and *Verse Daily*, and on National Public Radio. He is an associate professor, honors faculty, and chair of the English department at the College of St. Scholastica in Duluth, Minnesota.

**Connie Wanek** is the author of four poetry books: *Rival Gardens, Bonfire, Hartley Field*, and *On Speaking Terms*. She is coeditor of *To Sing Along the Way: Minnesota Women Poets from Pre-Territorial Days to the Present*. Wanek has been a Witter Bynner Fellow of the Library of Congress and was named George Morrison Artist of the Year, an honor given to a northern Minnesotan for contributions to the arts over many years.

**Michael Waters** is a 2017 Guggenheim Fellow. His recent books include *Caw* (BOA Editions), *The Dean of Discipline* (University of Pittsburgh Press), *Celestial Joyride* (BOA Editions), and a coedited anthology, *Border Lines: Poems About Migration* (Knopf). He lives in Ocean, New Jersey.

**Terin Weinberg** is an MFA candidate at Florida International University in Miami. She graduated with two BA degrees in environmental studies and English from Salisbury University in Maryland. She serves as the poetry editor for *Gulf Stream Magazine*. Her poetry has appeared in or is forthcoming from *The Normal School, Flyway: Journal of Writing & Environment, Red Earth Review*, and *Waccamaw*.

**Sarah Brown Weitzman**, a past National Endowment for the Arts Fellow in poetry and twice nominated for the Pushcart Poetry Prize, has had poems published in many journals and anthologies, including *New Ohio Review, North American Review, Rattle, Verse Daily, Mid-American Review, Poet Lore, Potomac Review, Miramar, Spillway*, and *The Antigonish Review*. Her books are available from Main Street Rag and Amazon.

**Connie Wieneke**'s work has appeared in *Stand, Pilgrimage, Whiskey Island Magazine, High Plains Register, Creative Nonfiction, Split Rock Review*, and the anthology *Artists Field Guide to Yellowstone* (Trinity Press). She holds an MFA in creative writing from the University of Montana and received two fellowships from the Wyoming Arts Council. When Wieneke isn't writing about the West and its various inhabitants, she focuses on family and memory.

**Sarah Wolfson** is the author of the poetry collection *A Common Name for Everything* (Green Writers Press). Her poems have appeared in Canadian and American journals, including *AGNI*, *TriQuarterly*, *Fiddlehead*, *Michigan Quarterly Review*, and *PRISM International*. Her work has been nominated for a Pushcart Prize and was named a notable poem in Best Canadian Poetry 2019. She holds an MFA from the University of Michigan. Originally from Vermont, she now lives in Montreal, where she teaches writing at McGill University.

# EDITOR

**Crystal S. Gibbins** is a Canadian-American writer; founder and editor of *Split Rock Review* and Split Rock Press; and author of *Now/Here* (Holy Cow! Press), winner of the 2017 Northeast Minnesota Book Award for poetry. She holds a PhD in English from the University of Nebraska–Lincoln and an MFA in creative writing from Minnesota State University Moorhead. Crystal is the recipient of grants from the Minnesota State Arts Board, Arrowhead Regional Arts Council, and Chequamegon Bay Arts Council. Her poetry and comics can be found in *Cincinnati Review*, *Coffee House Writers Project*, *Hobart*, *Minnesota Review*, *North American Review*, *Parenthesis Journal*, *Verse Daily*, *The Writer's Almanac*, and elsewhere. Originally from the Northwest Angle and Islands in Lake of the Woods (MN/ON), she now lives on the south shore of Lake Superior in northern Wisconsin. For more information, visit www.crystalgibbins.com.

## REVIEWERS

**Amy Clark** is the author of a memoir, *Remnants of the Disappeared,* and a graduate of the MFA Program in Creative Writing and Environment at Iowa State University. She has published poetry in various journals such as *Mid-American Review* and *Cimarron Review.* Amy moved to Duluth after being inspired by the "big lake," but now lives near the Boundary Waters Canoe Area Wilderness and is working on a collection of lyric essays that discuss the intersection of science, history, mythology, and a sulfide mine debate.

**Whitney (Walters) Jacobson** is an assistant professor at the University of Minnesota Duluth and an assistant editor of *Split Rock Review.* She holds an MFA in creative writing from Minnesota State University Moorhead. Her poetry and creative nonfiction have been published in *Punctuate, Feminine Collective, Up North Lit, After the Pause,* and *Wanderlust-Journal,* among others. Whitney is currently working on a collection of essays exploring skills, objects, and traits passed on (or not) from generation to generation.

**Andrew Jones** is an assistant professor of English and creative writing and coordinates the Archway Reading & Lecture Series at the University of Dubuque. His work has appeared in publications such as *Sierra Nevada Review, North American Review, Hobart,* and *Arroyo Literary Review,* among others. He lives with his wife and daughter in Dubuque, Iowa.

Poet, novelist, and nonfiction writer **Adrian Gibbons Koesters** holds an MFA in poetry from the Rainier Writing Workshop at Pacific Lutheran University and a PhD in fiction and poetry from the University of Nebraska–Lincoln, where she has taught creative writing. Her most recent work, the novel *Miraculous Medal,* was published in 2020 by Apprentice House Press. She lives in Omaha, Nebraska.

# CREDITS

Kelli Russell Agodon, "SOS" first appeared in *Glass: A Journal of Poetry*. Reprinted with permission of the author.

James Armstrong, "Oligotrophic" from *Blue Lash*, Milkweed Editions. Copyright © 2007 by James Armstrong. Reprinted with permission of the author.

Kimberly Blaeser, "Eloquence of Earth" from *Copper Yearning*, Holy Cow! Press. Copyright © 2019 by Kimberly Blaeser. Reprinted with permission of the author and publisher.

Elizabeth Bradfield, "Permeable" first appeared in *Kenyon Review*. Reprinted with permission of the author.

Nicholas Bradley, "Provincial Letter" from *Sweet Water: Poems for the Watersheds*, Caitlin Press. Copyright © 2020 Nicholas Bradley. Reprinted with permission of the author.

Fleda Brown, "Felled Tree" from *No Need of Sympathy*. Copyright © 2013 by Fleda Brown. Reprinted with the permission of the Permissions Company, Inc., on behalf of BOA Editions, Ltd., www.boaeditions.org.

Sarah Carey, "A Pileated Woodpecker Shares Where to Find God" first appeared in *SWIMM Every Day*. Reprinted with permission of the author.

Judith Chalmer, "Autumn" from *Minnow*, Kelsay Books. Copyright © 2020 by Judith Chalmer. Reprinted with permission of the author.

Robin Chapman, "Prairie Restoration" first appeared in *Cider Press Review*. Reprinted with permission of the author.

Paula Cisewski, "The Becoming Game" first appeared in *Posit*. Reprinted with permission of the author.

Susan Cohen, "Natural History" first appeared in *Southern Review*. "Where Will You Go When Things Get Worse?" first appeared in *Portside*. Both reprinted with permission of the author.

Anne Coray, "Mausoleum" first appeared in *Poems & Plays*. Reprinted with permission of the author.

(Minneapolis: Milkweed Editions, 2013). Copyright © 2013 by Sean Hill. Reprinted with permission from Milkweed Editions. www.milkweed.org

Marybeth Holleman, "Dispatch from Siberia" first appeared in *Ice Floe 2011: International Poetry of the Far North,* University of Alaska Press. "How to Grieve a Glacier" first appeared in *ISLE.* "Wing Feather" first appeared in *Cirque.* All reprinted with permission of the author.

Bethany Schultz Hurst, "Amelia Earhart, Rock Springs 1931" first appeared in *Narrative.* "Fruits of Our Labor" first appeared in *American Literary Review.* "Seascape with Evacuating Animals" first appeared in *Gulf Coast.* All reprinted with permission of the author.

Jen Karetnick, "Flight Plan" first appeared in *Passager Journal.* Reprinted with permission of the author.

Julia Spicher Kasdorf, "F-Word" from *Shale Play: Poems and Photographs from the Fracking Fields* by Julia Spicher Kasdorf and Steven Rubin. Copyright © 2018 by Julia Spicher Kasdorf. Reprinted with permission from Penn State University Press.

Benjamín Naka-Hasebe Kingsley, "Los Alamos, New Mexico: An Open Letter to Radiation Poisoning," from *Not Your Moma's Melting Post*, the Backwaters Press. Copyright © 2018 by Benjamín Naka-Hasebe Kingsley. Reprinted with permission of the author.

Jacqueline Kolosov, "Repair" first appeared in *Prairie Schooner.* Reprinted with permission of the author.

Ted Kooser, "Conch Shell" first appeared in *Antioch Review.* Reprinted with permission of the author.

Lance Larsen, "Aphorisms for a Lonely Planet," which sections first appeared in *Brevity, Laurel Review, Raritan, Short Circuits*, and *Southern Review.* "Compost" first appeared in *New Ohio Review.* Both reprinted with permission of the author.

Mercedes Lawry, "Biodiversity" first appeared in *Briar Cliff Review.* Reprinted with permission of the author.

Ada Limón, "Dandelion Insomnia" from *The Carrying* by Ada Limón (Minneapolis: Milkweed Editions, 2018). Copyright © 2018 by Ada Limón. Reprinted with permission from Milkweed Editions. www.milkweed.org

## ALSO FROM FLEXIBLE PRESS

### Home: An Anthology

**A collection of Minnesota-focused** short stories, memoir, and poetry: exploring hope and loss, promises kept and promises broken, in their own personal search for home.

### Lake Street Stories

**An anthology of 12 short stories by Twin Cities authors,** exploring themes of struggle and rebirth, immigration and social change, and community and challenges, all focused on south Minneapolis's main street.

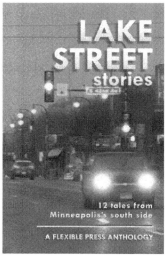

Made in the USA
Middletown, DE
07 September 2020

19070118R00146